Advance Praise for

Young People of the Pandemic

"I'm so thrilled to have my son be a part of this anthology."

—**Christina Chiu,** author of *Beauty*,
2020 James Alan McPherson Award winner

"We often wonder what our children are thinking. Nelson's collection offers a fascinating and honest understanding of how the pandemic affected them in their own voices. At turns sad and uplifting, painful and hopeful yet always a window into their minds and hearts."

—**Susan Newman, PhD,** social psychologist and
author of *Little Things Long Remembered:
Making Your Children Feel Special Every Day*

"The world has changed, moved on for good, and these are the important voices: the young people who will inherit the 'new normal.' This is wonderful reading, and a book that matters.

—**Bob Bickford,** author of *A Blueberry Moon for Corah*

"A book for our time, and for all time."

—**Gail Evans,** Emmy-nominated CNN Executive VP
and author of *Play Like a Man, Win Like a Woman*

Young People

of the

Pandemic

Young People

of the

Pandemic

An Anthology of Stories, Anecdotes, and Poems by 10- to 21-Year-Old Americans

Edited by NANCY S. NELSON, M.S., ATR
with SOPHIA LARSON
Chief Compiler, SOFIA HASKEL

ISBN: 978-0-578-77371-1 (Paperback)
ISBN: 978-0-578-77372-8 (Ebook)

First edition

For my young people of the pandemic:
Emma, Will, Maddy, Annie, and Teddy.

For Sophia Larson, who made this book possible.

CONTENTS

———

INTRODUCTION *by Nancy Nelson, Editor*   xi

CHAPTER I: *Our Youngest Writers: Ages 10 to 13*   1

     COMPILERS   3

         Samuel Eastaugh   3

         Josephine and Norah Caplan   6

         Teddy Cooper   11

         Hailey Koplowitz   14

         Gabriella Gonzalez   16

         Lena Lajko   18

     CONTRIBUTORS   21

CHAPTER II: *Our Mid-Teen Writers: Ages 14 to 17*   37

     COMPILERS   39

         James Yu   39

         Kaleigh Martin   42

         Lilith Freund   45

         Sophie Witherspoon   48

     CONTRIBUTORS   51

CHAPTER III: *Our Young Adult Writers: Ages 18 to 21*   95

    COMPILERS   97

       Sophia Larson, Assistant Editor   97

       Sofia Haskel, Chief Compiler   100

       Tess Haskel   104

       Nate Bickford   107

       Audrey Gabriel   111

       Christina Hohne   114

       Benjamin Katz   116

       Aidan Ferguson   117

    CONTRIBUTORS   119

CONCLUSION   155

ACKNOWLEDGMENTS   161

INTRODUCTION

The idea for this book came to me on March 17, 2020, after one week of isolation in my New York City apartment. I had been thinking of the thousands of pediatric and young adult clients, some healthy and some not, whom I had worked with over the past forty years in my capacity as a clinical art therapist. With COVID-19 encircling the country, I was concerned about my own family, many elderly friends, and the city where I'd lived for most of my life. But it was Gen Z (those born between 1995 and 2015) that I felt would be most impacted by this worldwide pandemic.

Having previously written two books, I nevertheless decided against writing about the crisis myself. Instead, my goal was to compile the stories, comments, poetry, and anecdotes of young people across the United States. By April 15, with the help of my personal contacts and a network of teachers, professors, fellow art therapists, and creative writing instructors, I had established a core group of eleven ten-to-twenty-one-year-olds who would be my compilers for this anthology. In just one day, my Facebook post helped recruit another six youngsters with referrals from strangers; parents, grandparents, aunts, and uncles who wanted their young relatives to participate in the book. From each compiler, I requested that they write two pieces within three months, and obtain written contributions from two friends living in states other than their own.

Sophia Larson from Massachusetts, a talented college freshman in her final month of online classes, agreed to be my Assistant Editor. By mid-May, we had obtained twenty-eight submissions and she created a sample cover from photographs of our compilers. We then began to contact a countrywide network of educators, childcare workers, and creative arts professionals in order to get more submissions. My intent was to only edit the written work for gross technical or grammatical errors because I wanted the contributors' words to be authentic.

On June 3, I conducted the first of several Zoom meetings with my compilers, whom I fondly refer to as "Team YPOP" (an acronym of the book title). At these meetings, we read submissions which shared the writers' experiences and reactions to the pandemic as it traveled across the country. In some meetings, I also gave writing prompts to obtain additional content for the book. The group's attendance varied with the twenty-one team members occasionally traveling to escape local outbreaks or to visit family, tending to jobs and volunteer obligations, and participating in camp or school activities. Another creative college freshman, Californian Sofia Haskel, soon became our Chief Compiler and was tasked with managing Team YPOP and designing our website and Instagram page.

Throughout the process of compilation, the initial goal was to perform a public service for a national population in crisis. For the writers and me, there was also the realization that we might be producing an historical record of how America's youth explained and managed the upheavals to our entire society. Online websites began to tell stories from active users, but these could not offer permanent documentation.

All ages of writers displayed a range of emotional reactions, much like what has been observed in adults. As someone who has worked with a varied socioeconomic and multicultural youth population, I found little disparity in expressive ability. With each group—ages 10 to 13 (Chapter I), 14 to 17 (Chapter II), and 18 to 21 (Chapter III)—concerns for personal and family survival, and our country's welfare, differed along age-appropriate lines. Content in the written pieces was dependent on what each person had witnessed or been exposed to. Some contributors were blessed not to know anyone who was ill, while others had relatives or friends who had been directly impacted.

My personal aim was to read each submission not from the eye of a therapist, but rather as an editor of courageous creative expression. In much the same way that a single drawing cannot be the totality of an art therapy judgement, I would never allow myself to form any diagnostic or predictive opinion based on one or two writing samples. However, what is commonly understood is the fact that all the arts— visual, performance, musical, and literary—are often utilized to ease trauma and express emotional tension. Art has long been a method of healing both physical and psychological difficulties. The ability to EX-press rather than DE-press is a wonderful attribute during this time of personal and collective trauma. I strongly believe that the content of this book displays a resilient youth population whose words can be admired as a source of healing and motivation.

At the beginning of each chapter are the works of my compilers, followed by submissions written by additional contributors. In every submission there is a voice that needs to be heard. In most of the writing, there is also an element of hope, even in those pieces that describe the sadness of personal loss or the anger at current events. We received no written work that contained inappropriate language, and very few that expressed political bias. With the onset of the national Black Lives Matter protests, many of our compilers and contributors attended these events. As a result of their participation in this move-ment, the literary voices of these young writers became more insistent, and their opinions quite realistic. From thirteen-year-old twins who protested in Washington to a twenty-year-old California political vol-unteer, the many descriptions of the country's tumultuous atmosphere are remarkable. To predict how the future worldview of this young population will be shaped by these times is anybody's guess.

A primary goal in compiling this anthology was to present a wide spectrum of experiences and responses to the worldwide pandemic. Of equal importance was to obtain a glimpse into the writers' internal lives while in the midst of external turmoil. The book contains work that is both heartbreaking and heartwarming. There are amusing anec-dotes, unusual poetic formats, as well as long stories. Submissions were chosen with an attempt to represent a literary and geographical variety.

While editing this book, I became increasingly confident that Gen Z will bring this country, and the world, into a better place. It is my hope that you, the reader, will also find inspiration in these pages.

—Nancy Nelson, Editor

CHAPTER I

Our Youngest Writers:
Ages 10 to 13

Under normal circumstances, the tween years are a time of growing independence mingled with uncertainty, as many children still require parental guidance and reassurance. It is a period of rapid change, both on the exterior developing body and in the interior thought process. In ordinary times, kids aged 10 to 13 can, seemingly overnight, go from little children to new and different people.

It seems the pandemic has possibly accelerated these changes. During the upheavals created by the virus, these children have had to rapidly learn to tolerate and regulate emotions that most adults can barely grapple with. The content of this chapter's writing contains descriptions of close family ties, attachments to pets, and reliance on teachers and peers. There are stories of being "extra nice" to a sibling, showing appreciation for a teacher, the newfound joy of having a pet, and love for socially distanced friends. There is also fear of illness, sadness for lost relatives, and feelings of loneliness. Some poignant yet revealing examples include a story of sad anticipation for a milestone birthday which turned out to be fun, a letter to healthcare workers acknowledging fear while expressing gratitude, a short piece about the death of close relatives who are reunited in heaven, and an insightful and amusing list of what to do in quarantine. Each written piece in this chapter represents a fascinating microcosm of an individual coping with a worldwide crisis.

For some pre-teen and early teen writers, there is the expression of boredom, particularly among those accustomed to being pro-grammed with many extracurricular activities. There are many stories of missing their sports, team and individual competitions, and various other after-school activities. These youth have been participating in such programs from a very young age, while supportive parents have also been quite used to the time and travel involved. In other families, youngsters have been encouraged to spend more time in soli-tary pursuits. Therefore, some of the written works reveal interests in doing crafts, writing poetry, or other individual activities such as hiking. Regardless of these variances, most contributors—even the youngest—display an awareness of the pandemic having initiated an unfamiliar way of living.

By age 13, while importance is still placed on family, friends, and one's own life, there develops a strong interest in outside events as well. For instance, many stories were submitted about observing or attending protests. Some described seeing changes in their neighbor-hoods, such as the erection of medical tents in a local parking lot, the limited number of customers in an ice cream shop, or unusual experiences with distancing from friends. The clarity of thought dem-onstrated in their writing is particularly remarkable for young lives that have become so disorganized. As in later chapters, there are some precocious writers with advanced vocabularies and sentence struc-ture. But there is also a variety in writing styles, along with a wide degree of emotional capacity to describe the effects of living through such difficult times.

As the summer of 2020 set in, there were fewer submissions in this age group due to some US states lifting restrictions. This allowed for the reopening of sports and recreation classes, camps, and extracur-ricular and outdoor activities, all of which are vitally important for youth whose restlessness and pent-up energy are hallmarks of this age range. For their parents, there was some relief from dealing with the behaviors of tweens who have been cooped up for too long. Despite the hardships of isolation, quarantine, and social distancing, the kids who contributed to this first chapter showed an amazing amount of resilience, as can be seen in so much of their writing. What is most striking is that, during a short time period of having to grow up too fast, so many have adapted despite such unusual and devastat-ing events.

COMPILERS: AGES 10 TO 13

Samuel Eastaugh, 12
(Fort Lauderdale, Florida)

Submission 1: March 2, 2020

It is day 46 of quarantine. I am so bored. And I miss my sports. If I have to do this one more week, I will go crazy. It is crazy out. Everyone is wearing masks at the supermarket. I am lucky I am with my mom and dad. Some people are alone. But...I'm bored, I'm bored, I'm bored, I'm bored, I'm bored, I'm bored, I'm bored, I'm bored, I'm bored, I'm bored. I wrote it ten times.

Submission 2: June 2, 2020

It is the fourth month of staying at home due to COVID-19 and I am just finishing the school year online. Home school has not been completely awful. I wake up early and get all my work done in the morning, then have time to do other things in the afternoon. The difficult part is that you do not get to see any of your friends. You only get to see them in online meetings.

The worst part of the pandemic has been that all sports were canceled during this time. You couldn't play or watch any sports. I finally started doing private lessons for water polo, two days a week. The coaches say that we are going back in a few weeks. My dad and I have also been going out surfing a lot. The beaches are finally open and there has been good surf!! No one can sunbathe yet, but you are allowed to swim and surf for fitness.

At night, I go for a walk with my family and my friend Andreas' family. The whole walk, Andreas and I throw the football and look for things to jump over. We try to do as much as we can while out because we are cooped up in our houses all day and just need to let loose.

I am looking forward to the summer. They say lifeguard camp may be on in July, which I do every year. Things are getting a lot better in Florida. Now you can go into shops and stores, but you still have to wear a facemask and social distance. I remember before, when the stores and beaches were all closed. I'm very happy those times are slowly going away.

Submission 3: July 3, 2020

Everything has been changing. First, we had to switch to homeschool, next we went into lockdown mode, and then they closed the beaches by our house. Dad and I heard good surf was coming, and we decided to head to Fort Pierce for the day before they shut their beaches down. Mom was not sure about it, but we needed to get out of the house and do something that felt normal. She packed us everything under the moon to keep us safe. Gloves, masks, hand sanitizer, big sandwiches, and snacks so we would not have to stop.

We were able to get a couple of early sets in with our friends in Fort Pierce before the police came and asked us to leave on their loudspeakers. It felt so nice to paddle out in the crystal blue ocean and have no stress at all. There were such good waves that day, and there were surfers in the water that haven't surfed in months. It was as if COVID-19 was not a thing that day.

They sent police boats out and towed the cars, but luckily we had parked at our friend's house, so we did not have to get out of the ocean straight away. We could enjoy just a few more waves before they shut us down. The police were driving four-wheelers up and down the beach, asking people to leave. I do not know why they wanted to close it down, as everyone had enough space and only surfers were out in the ocean. The ocean felt so good and it was a great day out with Dad. We had no stress or fears, just us and the ocean.

Afterwards I went with my friends to our favorite sandwich shop, Sharky's, and got some food. It was so different up north because nobody wore masks or worried about COVID-19. It was not bad at all up there. It felt nice not having to worry about the pandemic, and just having a normal time. By the time we got onto the highway, I was fast asleep in the car. I woke up back at my house where the dream day was over. This was definitely one of the best times I was able to have in quarantine so far.

Sam will be entering seventh grade in the fall of 2020. During the spring coronavirus outbreak, he especially missed his water sports; he is on a South Florida water polo team. With an Australian-born dad, he has surfed in Costa Rica and Puerto Rico. Sam, therefore, can be called a grom, or surfer dude.

Josephine and Norah Caplan, 13 (Washington, DC)

Submission 1: May 7, 2020

"Mom and Dad, can we please, please, PLEASE have a dog?" This is what we have been saying to our parents since the age of five, yet we always received the same answer, despite our persuasive efforts. Our thirteenth birthday was the date that we had agreed upon, the date when our new best friend was destined to enter our household. We would constantly go on walks and watch other dogs frolic with their owners, and we waited enthusiastically when that time would come for us. Our mom had always been the one pushing back on the idea of adopting yet another pet, in addition to our cat. Who knew that it would take schools and restaurants all over the world to close until our mom would be persuaded.

That Friday, everyone went to school like normal. We had all been informed that our school was starting spring break a month early and that we would return to school in just a week or two. Every class that day seemed to go the exact same way.

"Hello everyone," our teachers would say, "Today we are just going to go over the procedure if school is…" Canceled. Postponed. Virtual. There wasn't a single person at Hardy Middle School who had any idea what was coming. The one thing that no one could get was facts, and that is exactly what everyone wanted.

That night at dinner, our mom told everyone that she wanted to go to an adoption event the next day. We all took that news as normal; it seemed as though we had gone to thousands of adoption events in the course of three months. The one thing they all had in common was that we returned empty-handed. But Saturday turned out to be the day our family changed "furever"!

The day we adopted our new family member, Pepper Corona, from her shelter, Homeward Trails, was a surreal moment. The thought of actually getting a dog hadn't seemed like a reality until we walked into the doors of that shelter. There was a pretty big crowd and our hearts swelled with the fact that we might find our forever friend today. A man came up to us and told us that he was going to help us find a dog.

"We are going to find a dog," we said to ourselves, our hearts beating in anticipation.

The man came out with a black and white lab. "This is Sadie," he told us.

Sadie walked up to me and licked my palm, causing us to laugh. We took a purple striped rope lying on the ground and waved it in front of her face. Our mom was not into Sadie. Apparently, she was too big and energetic. We both thought we were going to come home empty-handed. Then, Pepper came into the room, very timid and shy, but her spirit completely won us over. She walked over to Dad and jumped on him, licking him all over and jumping to get in his lap. We all started laughing. She ran from Mom to Dad and then back to us, licking all of us while she was at it. It felt like Pepper Corona was a part of our family from that moment on. We drove home with a dog lying next to us. Our whole family was on cloud nine. It seemed like, in spite of the world today, there is a reason to hope and love. "Happiness is a choice." That is what our dad says every day we are upset, sad, or angry with the world. Our whole family is so glad that we chose happiness by getting Pepper.

A couple of weeks later, the tentative dog we met at the shelter completely blossomed into herself. Pepper fit into our family lifestyle perfectly, like a puzzle piece we never knew was lost. We all developed a new way of life anyway since COVID-19, and Pepper really helped our family have many laughs over this horrible time. She sleeps in her crate and we don't hear from her the whole night. When we wake up in the morning, we get Pepper out of her crate and then sit down so she can throw her body on us and give us love. She doesn't have a tail, so her whole butt wiggles the minute someone unlocks her crate.

Our cat, Murray Sparkles Rainbow Cat Caplan, has learned to coexist with Pepper very well. They both wait for us to come home when we go outside to play soccer. One of us pets Murray while the other is with Pepper. It feels like our family is complete.

"Pepper is going to be so upset when we all get back to our normal routine," our dad always says, laughing as Pepper jumps on him after only forty-five minutes apart. No one in our family knew just how long it would be before we would go back to school. We still have no idea. Pepper has brought so much joy to our lives, but the not knowing anything about our future has made us all very stressed. Meanwhile, Pepper Corona is living the best doggy life ever. COVID-19 has made her be in heaven. Every day, there is anticipation, anxiety, sadness, and worry in this house, but we just have to remind ourselves of the good. Our family is healthy, we are safe, and we rescued a dog's life who has brought so much unexpected joy into ours. Everyone out there reading this, adopt an animal! You, just like us, will be very grateful you did, especially in these dark times.

Submission 2: July 7, 2020

"Black lives matter! Black lives matter!" The thundering sound of protestors echoed through the streets of Washington, DC, the sound seeming to reach people a million miles away. We craned our necks over the thousands of people in order to see a glimpse of the new Black Lives Matter Plaza. Everywhere you looked, there were people wearing masks, holding signs declaring their anger and frustration, and we were there too, fighting for our rights despite of COVID-19, like everyone else.

People lined the streets all over the world that day. After the murder of George Floyd, anger swept the country like a herd of angry bees swarming around a beehive. America was standing up from all the inequality, and we were there, with everyone in DC, right outside of the White House, making our voices heard.

It seemed incredible that after months of isolation people refused to be silenced by the fear of sickness. The fight for equality for African Americans has been happening for centuries, and people have been ignoring blatant injustices since the birth of America. People need to realize that African Americans should have been seen as equals 244 years ago, the year that America was founded. The fact that thousands of people all over the world came out to protest amidst a pandemic proves how urgent the need is to end police brutality.

All the shops around us were barricaded. Cardboard covered everything, making DC, the nation's capital, feel like a ghost town. There were fences put up a block away from the White House, trying to protect the president. Thousands of people used to roam the streets over there, and now it is blocked off, leaving us staring at the wide empty streets, trying to remember what DC used to look like, what it should look like. As we biked closer to the people, we felt a tingle of fear creep up our spines. What if the military would come out and use teargas to make us leave? No one should ever feel the fear of raising your voice. Just thinking about it made us realize the horrible state America is in.

All of this anger, boarded streets, military tanks across the city, is not America. This is not the country where people come to have the American dream. We are ashamed to live in America right now. Ashamed to see all of this hurt. This is not who we are. We are better than this. It is sickening that George Floyd got killed. We don't know what to do with ourselves anymore. A kid should never have to have these thoughts go through their head.

There shouldn't even be protests during COVID right now. George Floyd, and all the others should have never been killed in the first place. It is sickening to think that policemen don't make us feel as safe anymore. Walking into the streets, we are afraid. We are afraid but are ready to make our voices heard. We are ready to show the world the thing that makes America America: the ability to speak out, to make our voices heard.

So, everyone who went out to raise their voice, thank you. It is beyond courageous to go out into the streets to fight for what you believe in while risking your health. In this strange and scary time, it is easy to be swept aside by grief and anger. By raising your voice during this pandemic, you are helping shape our country's future. We will never forget the sea of masks that came together during this time. Although a mask may cover your face, our voices refuse to be silenced, and never will be as long as America stands.

Norah and Josephine are twin sisters, who are seventh graders at a Washington, DC public school. They are passionate soccer players, inspired by the US Women's National team. Their bat mitzvah, including a large party, was held on November 16, 2019. Many Jewish American children had their winter and spring 2020 bar and bat mitzvahs canceled due to coronavirus. The girls' mother is a journalist in Washington.

Photo with Pepper Corona
courtesy of Julianna Caplan.

Teddy Cooper, 13
(West Harrison, New York)

Submission 1: May 10, 2020

The moment that I realized the extent of this pandemic was when I was driving with my dad along the Bronx River Parkway. I saw something that I have never seen before, which was the parking lot and building of the Westchester County Center full of rows of medical tents. Fearless healthcare workers were treating the sick patients of Westchester. Just a few weeks earlier, I was at that very arena, and now, it was serving as a hospital for the victims of the COVID-19 pandemic.

Then I realized that this disease was no joke and is the most devastating disease of my life, and possibly of all time. Now that everything is on hold and everyone is at home, I've been able to realize how that one moment helped me grasp what was going on throughout the world.

Submission 2: June 16, 2020

I know that at this point it may seem like a cliché, but I believe that during this quarantine everyone has learned something new. During this unique past school year of online learning, I was able to have a firsthand experience that even our teachers have as much to learn as us students. After one class of mine, where we had an independent assignment, I felt that I had not performed to the best of my abilities for the simple reason that I had more distractions accessible to me than ever before, which distracted me from my work that day. Since I felt that I could have done better, I decided to tell my teacher the truth, which was that I had been exposed to more distractions than at any given moment that I had faced during all of my time in school. The response that I received from that teacher was very different from what I had expected. Instead of shaming me for not being able to focus on my work, that teacher was able to take from my email that it was

hard for children and adults alike to stay motivated during this difficult time. This teacher then told me that, based on my experience, she
had learned to empathize with her students in the future, specifically
during an unpredictable time.

I learned from this experience both that what I say can impact
how someone else views the world, as well as that I should always be
sincere because it can end up being rewarding for me. This teacher's
response also allowed me to reflect on how just from being honest
I may have been able to change another student's experience in the
future. Even though I had my doubts about telling my teacher the
truth, in the end I can reflect on the decision and realize how my
choice benefited me and others. I appreciate how my teacher reacted
to my decision and I want people to know that she helped teach me
a very powerful lesson.

Submission 3: July 1, 2020

Spring training for all major league baseball teams begins today. After
months of deciding if a 2020 season could be salvaged, and if players and
owners could agree on salaries, opening day is now expected on July 23.
Each team will play 60 games, whereas a regular season is 162 games.

Because of coronavirus, both the American and National leagues
will be playing against their own regional teams, i.e. eastern division
plays eastern teams, west against west, and central versus central. This
prevents the usual extensive travel crisscrossing the country, so players
will not have to spend so much time on planes and trains. There will
be no fans in the stadiums, which could certainly influence the players
and the play.

There are some players concerned about playing ball and going
home to pregnant wives, along with other health-related issues. The
leagues are discussing a special injury list to accommodate such concerns. While there may be favorite players absent from the field at
times, most of the nation's fans are ecstatic to see the return of baseball to the TV screen, hopefully concluding with the playoffs on
September 29. The World Series is set to begin on October 20 with a
potential game seven to be played on October 27.

Like many baseball fans, I am happy that the players held out for
prorated salaries which the teams could well afford. After all, the
owners are billionaires while the players are only millionaires!

Teddy is a seventh-grade student who lives in Westchester County, the location of the first major outbreak in New York state. His school is located in the town of Rye, which is within eight miles of New Rochelle where community contact was widespread. Teddy volunteers with a local wheelchair basketball team. He is a lefty pitcher in Little League who hopes to someday play for the New York Yankees.

Photos of medical tents by
Teddy Cooper.

Hailey Koplowitz, 13 (Califon, New Jersey)

Submission 1

It was just an ordinary snowy December Friday. I was eager for the bell to ring, so I could finally go home. Last period on Fridays were usually boring in science because of current event presentations. I was dazed, barely able to function. The last current event was finally being presented. It was about the coronavirus in China. For once during that class, my eyes were not glued to the clock. My head immediately turned to the boy presenting. I vividly remember hearing about a virus in China, which was deadly and rapidly spreading. The bell finally rang, and I dashed out of the classroom to my locker.

I had not again heard or thought of the virus until mid-January. Until then, no one took it seriously. On January 22, the first reported case of coronavirus was announced. I remember my classmates and I watching the news during last-period science. We could not believe our eyes; we were all in disbelief. Day by day, the cases kept climbing at a slow pace, then increasing rapidly. I was going on vacation February 11, to my vacation house in Arizona. We bought masks to wear at the airport, but no one in sight was wearing them. We never wore masks until March 11. It was a school field trip to New York City, to see a Broadway play. We were prohibited by teachers to wear masks on the trip. They claimed no one was going to catch the virus. My brother and I both brought one just in case. During that time, it was considered being an outcast to society by wearing one. The very next day, they shut down Broadway, along with many other things in New York. People finally started to realize how bad of an illness this was becoming. It was becoming a pandemic.

On March 13, my whole school was scrambling to prepare for an emergency closure. The governor still had not announced for public schools to close, though it was anticipated. It was third period, when an announcement came onto the loudspeaker: "Attention all staff and students, due to the coronavirus, the governor has announced a two-week school closure effective Monday, March 16." Everyone began scrambling to their lockers at the end of the day, packing all of the stuff in they could fit. It was mayhem. We all thought we would be back on March 21. That Friday was my last day of eighth grade, my last day of middle school, my last day of normalcy.

Submission 2

I was lying in bed on a rainy April Friday. Almost every state in the country had announced school was closed, with the exception of New Jersey. I was eager to find out the fate of my eighth-grade year. I had hoped school would resume in late-May. The time came for the governor's 1 p.m. press conference that I closely listened to daily. On that Friday, he announced all schools would stay closed through the end of the year. I felt defeated. All the countless hours studying, all the hard work I put into assignments, all I had ever worked for, everything was gone. I had always dreamt of how my eighth grade DC trip would go or what I would wear to graduation. Those dreams never came true.

Hailey is an incoming freshman at Pope John High School in Sparta, New Jersey. She loves to travel and explore the outdoors. One of her favorite outdoor activities is hiking. Hailey also loves clothes and fashion.

Gabriella Gonzalez, 10
(Rye Brook, New York)

Submission 1: June 18, 2020

I was going to celebrate my tenth birthday with my friends at a Ninja Warrior gym, but then quarantine came. I felt sad and thought I would have a boring, lonely birthday because I couldn't be with my friends. Soon, my birthday came. I was having a birthday car parade! When it was finally time for the car parade, I went outside. I saw my friends' cars lined up. They were honking their horns and driving on my street past my house. My face had a huge smile. The neighbors came out too! There was cheering, clapping, birthday signs, balloons, cards, and gifts. My family was there, and my grandma took a video of the whole parade. It was much more fun, exciting, and special than I had expected. I will always remember how awesome my tenth birthday was during the COVID-19 pandemic.

Submission 2: July 10, 2020

Q-U-A-R-A-N-T-I-N-E

Quiet times during the days of COVID-19
Understand social distance to stay safe
An absolute crazy time
Remote Zooms for school learning and with friends
A time to bake and eat sweet treats
Never touching or hugging friends
There are still bright days ahead
I hope in the coming weeks and months
No going to friends' houses or public places
Enjoy thinking of the end of the COVID-19 pandemic!

Gabriella completed fourth grade at a Westchester County, New York public school. She was able to attend her sleepaway camp in Maine, which opened in the beginning of July for a five-week session. She lives with her parents and sister and loves sea turtles. She especially enjoys drawing, biking, and swimming.

Lena Lajko, 12
(Fort Lauderdale, Florida)

Submission 1: May 20, 2020

During quarantine, many things have changed, including the delay of sporting events and practices. I am a swimmer, and this tragic turn of events deeply impacted me.

In the middle of March, I had the most important swimming competition a twelve-year-old swimmer could have had. It was the Florida Gold Coast Junior Olympics, where I was ranked top five in most of my events. I had been training for this event six times a week, two hours a day, twelve hours a week, since November 2019. Just to qualify for this meet and have to be ranked top five I had to compete at eight meets in the season. The competition was supposed to begin on March 13 and end on March 15. That is three whole days of prelims and finals. I was scheduled to swim seven individual events and four relays.

I was ready. I have never been a reader for a swim meet in my whole life. I was physically and mentally prepared. I knew I was ready to win, and nothing could hold me back.

It was March 12, the day before the Junior Olympics. My two swim bags were packed by the front door, ready for my big day, my big weekend. I packed my warm-up suit, my warm-up goggles, and my competition tech suit, brand new, never worn before. My parka, my five towels, I had everything I needed to feel ready for the meet.

At around 3 p.m. I got the most heartbreaking email from my coach: the Junior Olympics were canceled.

I was heartbroken. I didn't understand why, didn't understand how, and didn't understand how a virus can affect people so badly.

At first, I panicked, then I was angry, all while feeling disappointed. When you are stuck in a place where you think that all the hard work you put in to achieve whatever goal you had set for yourself is gone, well, think again, my friend. Not all hope is lost.

This tragic turn of events made me strive even more to work hard to achieve my goals. I don't take anything for granted anymore. From one moment to another, I lost a lot of things I took for granted. I lost the chance to compete at a meet, my everyday swim practice, and my swim friends.

But I had to stay strong and focus on my goals, which were not lost. What is more, I saw them clearer than before. I switched to tethered swimming in our home pool. Every day, I swam alone for an hour, counting my own strokes. It was anything but fun, yet I knew I was fortunate to be able to stay in shape while a lot of my fellow swim pals didn't feel the water for months.

I want to compete again, I want to feel that jitter, the adrenaline in my body. Hopefully, I will be able to hit the wall soon.

Submission 2: July 9, 2020

It was 9:02 a.m. and I took a look at my email inbox. It was flooded with emails from school. I just wanted to cry, break my laptop in half. I can't do this, and even if I can, I don't want to. Everybody was talking about this as "homeschooling". I didn't think it was homeschooling; homeschooling was a choice, the student and her parents' choice. This was not our choice! We were forced into this.

I had tears in my eyes, I already felt defeated by homeschooling even before it had started. When I realized that it was 9:05 a.m. and I still had to attend my Zoom math meeting, I decided it was best if I finally opened the Zoom app and joined the meeting.

The math class was a mess, mostly because of my bad state of mind. I had a difficult time trying to comprehend what my teacher was trying to say. Something about dividing mixed fractions? Some of my other peers were too tired and they forgot to turn their microphone off, so the background noise would blend in with my teacher's explanation and it sounded like mumbo-jumbo.

As I was finishing up my math assignments, I looked in my inbox and there again were countless amounts of emails. They were all related to graded assignments, assignments I need to complete, graded tests, and threatening deadlines.

I tried to prioritize by deadline, by subject, and just stay afloat and breathe. Although I was at home far away from what I thought was my stress source, the school, I had never felt more worried and helpless.

By 2 p.m. I was so exhausted that I needed to take a break. I had an hour of swimming, which was super calming; just me and the water, no school, no to-do list, no deadlines.

Another three long hours of rushing through school stuff and I still wasn't done for the day? How was that even possible? I felt that this workload was enormous and simply unachievable in a day.

When I had completed my final assignment (or so I thought) and turned it in, I decided to hit the hay. As I was lying in bed, I was recalling all the assignments to see if I had completed all of them. Then, I suddenly realized that I forgot one assignment. I checked the time: 11:06 p.m. I had fifty-four minutes to complete a five-paragraph essay for my religion class!

During those fifty-four minutes, I had typed like I had never typed before. I had done the quickest revising and editing the human eye had ever seen. When I had finally completed the assignment, I checked the time: 11:59 p.m. I had sixty seconds left to turn in this assignment. As I did, the clock just ticked 12:00 a.m. and I could breathe and relax again.

Then, as I was finally resting my head, I told myself that tomorrow I would be ready to take on homeschooling.

Lena lives in Fort Lauderdale, Florida with her parents and younger brother. Born in Budapest, Hungary, she was eight months old when her family moved to the United States. Lena learned to swim when she was three years old, and since then she hasn't stopped practicing the sport she loves. Lena started competing at six and she won more medals than she can count. Some of them are small victories, but some of them are Florida Gold Coast titles.

CONTRIBUTORS (AGES 10 TO 13)

Emily McCarthy, 13
(Mesa, Arizona)

A Letter to my Good Friend, COVID-19

Dear COVID-19,

As you know, we've been stuck inside for months now. And I must say, it's like the most fun I've ever had. (Insert dramatic eye roll here.) It's amazing! Canceled shows, camps, and even better, no social interaction! I never thought I'd miss the absolute internal panic and chaos that comes with walking up to someone and introducing yourself. So much of my day has just consisted of me staring at my iPad, trying to come up with something to write. But, of course, as I haven't had much variety in my day (rehearsals, stores, restaurants, etc.), writer's block has taken over. Absolutely. Thrilling.

Other than the boredom that ensues when you're stuck in the same place all day, I actually have learned some valuable things that I can carry into my teen/adult years. First of all, I'm one of the people who can say I've lived through a pandemic like this. After this pandemic is over, children will be born into a new, post-pandemic world that we haven't seen since the Spanish Flu in 1918. But, unlike 1918's Spanish Flu, we're lucky enough to have things like electronic devices. I've also started to learn how to bake, which I doubt I would have done if you hadn't caused all this. Of course, I can't thank you for that. Really, I can't.

It's so much of an honor to be living history and, at the same time, so incredibly infuriating. Together (while very much apart), we plan to murder your face for the rest of forever. So, thank you, COVID-19. For absolutely nothing.

Love, Emily

Courtesy of Crystal Bowden, *Clothed Mole Rat Magazine*

Sonali Dhanidina, 13 (Irvine, California)

Masked Figures

Walking around,
seeing smiling faces,
caused major mistakes,
oh how the tables have turned.
Identities hidden,
behind sewed up cloths,
if only sooner we learned.
Anxious and bored,
trapped,
I never knew you could feel so alone.
When you pass by a stranger,
you will never know if you passed by an angel,
or a devil below.
But behind all those masks,
a wall of the unknown,
is someone like you who thinks they're alone.
Show them that standing there right by their side,
is a masked figure who is all pure inside.

Leonora Monteverde, 11 (Bethlehem, Pennsylvania)

Some Good Things about the Pandemic

1. When I go to school from home, I can take breaks, go outside when I want, and eat snacks whenever I want.
2. I get to spend more time with my family. I get to see my sister more, who goes to high school.
3. I like doing FaceTime with friends. It's almost like being with them.
4. I learned to use my parents' Apple computer. And when the virus is over, they said they are going to buy me one.
5. I taught my dog to lie down and roll over. It's fun to watch him do it.
6. I can chew gum all day if I want to.
7. I can go to the kitchen and get cookies whenever I want to.
8. I go outside to shoot hoops five times a day.
9. I don't have to deal with school lunches, which suck.
10. I get to watch more TV and play more video games.

Devon Richmond, 10 (New Castle, Delaware)

I never wrote anything for a book before this. But my mom said I should do it because kids in the pandemic are making history. I am not sure what she means. Maybe when I'm old I'll know what she meant. All I want to know now is when will I be able to play with my soccer team?

Sabrina, 10
(Rye, New York)

Coronavirus has given me a new perspective on myself. I realized that I was being mean to a black kid, and not knowing I was being really racist. Soon after, I found out about the protests and I started to feel upset. "Why is life so not fair?" I keep asking myself. "Black people should have the same rights as white people do."

I keep looking back on that day, seeing myself being racist, and I know I will NEVER do it again. Then I started to worry. I saw on TV some people in the protest were not even wearing masks! I was afraid of getting close to my friends, so I was almost convinced to self-isolate. My friends and I have gotten into fights about social, or more like physical, distancing. I felt that they were too close to each other, but I knew they thought they were the perfect distance. But as the days went by, and the numbers of coronavirus went down, I loosened up a little more. We started rainbow-loom bracelet companies. Baby-sitting companies. Group chats on iMessage. I made my own news-paper. Hangouts in friends' backyards with sprinklers, water slides, and frozen yogurt. Friday fun nights with pizza and cornhole. We met new friends and got their numbers. Slowly, the fights ceased. I'm also really glad that coronavirus numbers have gone down because my parents were letting relatives come over often into the house, so if they wanted to stay for dinner, they could eat inside of the house. The pandemic has also helped me explore new places. My mom got beach passes to a beach I have never been to before, and so did all my friends. We got to play at the beach together! I have also gone to The Kensico Dam with my sister. It is beautiful to go to new places.

I miss being able to go to school and I had great plans to go to my first year at Eagle Hill sleepaway camp, but it was sadly canceled. After we found out about camp, my family decided to rent a house with a pool for the summer, but then canceled it and used the money to redo our backyard.

I hope everything gets better soon.

Emma Faulkner, 10
(Henderson, Nevada)

My grandpa died of the virus a few weeks ago. He couldn't have a funeral because everyone was in quarantine, so the family had to stay in their own houses.

My older brother told me that COVID-19 is bad for old people who have other illnesses. I know Grandpa had asthma, just like I do. Both of us used the same kind of inhaler. Sometimes my asthma gets worse when I get scared, so the doctor and my parents try to make me calm. I guess I have to stop being scared so much.

Annabelle Babbington, 10
(Baton Rouge, Louisiana)

I go to my classes in a place called Zoom
My teacher's in a computer, not in her room.
Our house is where I now go to school,
But I do not think this is very cool.
The coronavirus is such an awful pain
To get a cure is the doctors' only aim.
Being at home so long is really boring.
I ask if the sickness is gone every morning
Because I think we'll all go crazy one day
Unless the COVID-19 soon goes away.
It is June and the weather has turned so hot
To breathe fresh air is long forgot.

Anne Whitmyer, 11
(Scarborough, Maine)

I live in a place where we don't have much coronavirus. But it's summertime and Maine is usually more crowded than it is this year. I often go into Portland with my family to do some shopping. The streets there are not as crowded with tourists as they are in most summers. I like to visit our ice cream parlors; now only two people at a time are allowed in. I feel sorry for the people from big cities in other states that have huge numbers of the virus. I can't imagine how scared those kids must be.

Shira Ehrlich, 13
(San Diego, California)

I must say, 2020 has been quite the roller coaster, but for me it hasn't been one that goes upside down or has quick turns and steep drops. During quarantine I have just felt like my roller coaster has stopped, and I don't fully know the extent of the problem, but I have hope that it will start up again, however much time it may take. I'm generally an optimistic person. I like to see the best in things and for problems to be solved, so I normally try to stay away from the news and distract myself with things I like to do. For example, I've started playing the piano more, tried to teach myself guitar, started a sketchbook to be more creative, and other things like that. What I have realized, though, is that if I leave myself time to think about the world today and things that have happened, I find myself subconsciously focusing on the negative because there isn't really much positive influence around me, especially because every time I go on social media I see that thousands of lives have been ridden with grief and frustration because nobody can do anything about the things that plague them. However much the events of today have affected people around the globe, I keep in mind that things do get better, and this too shall pass. It's difficult to stay grounded, but time still goes on, and in the future, I have hope that the passengers on this broken roller coaster will find their way to the relief that meets them at the end.

Marcus, 13
(Tulsa, Oklahoma)

The thing I like about staying home and going to school on the computer is that you don't have to be excused to go pee.

Jasper Anderson, 11
(Jackson Hole, Wyoming)

What is it?

It is a tricky virus.
It is something that doesn't like soap and water.
It is a sickness that doctors cannot fix.
It is something old people can die of.
It is like a bad cold for kids.
It is not anything Chinese.
It is all over the world.
It is not being cured soon.
It is necessary to wear masks.

It is not good we are out of school.
It is good we have computers.
It is better to stay home.
It is best to not be with lots of people.
It is going to get a vaccine.

Tabitha Debraski, 13 (Neshanic Station, New Jersey)

During quarantine, I've been seeing my cats almost all the time. Before this, my friendly cat, Liesl, would always walk up to my dad or brother, never me. But after eighty-one days stuck in the house with them, I know how to get her to like me. From nine to eleven in the morning, Liesl is usually tired, on my parent's bed. She is really friendly in the mornings and is okay with me holding her and petting her. Her favorite thing is when someone rubs her face, or she gets to rub her face on a corner. After a few minutes, she has already fallen asleep on me. Unfortunately, nine to eleven is the time that I'm working on school, so I have to wake her up and leave, which breaks my heart. Then I give her treats, so it's okay.

Being quarantined has made me know my cats pretty well, but I still have experiences with them that shock me. For example, I was cuddling with Liesl, and she licked me! The cats haven't licked my hand since I was five, so I was shocked! Her tongue felt like sandpaper, which I wasn't too surprised about. She licked my finger a few times, and then, to my surprise and horror, she licked her butt! I was disgusted because this made me realize she probably had done this before, meaning her butt germs were on my hand.

Another time Liesl surprised me was at five in the morning. I wasn't feeling well, and couldn't fall asleep, and who did I see but Liesl. She came into my room and sat by my window. Then she came over and just snuggled with me. For two hours, she went back and forth between me and the window. It was super nice and made me feel better.

Anyway, I wanted to be fair and include a story about my other cat, Sweetie. We have a bay window in our kitchen, and our cat beds are there. We also have a ton of bird feeders that you can see from the window, as well as window feeders. Now my cat Sweetie purrs very loudly, like REALLY loudly. She also makes really funny meows when my dog comes over to her. So, I already thought she made funny sounds. But recently, during quarantine, I've heard her meow totally differently. It sounds like she is talking to the birds because she makes little chirp sounds, like words.

It's obvious that a lot of bad things have happened because of the coronavirus, but getting to know my cats better is not one of them.

Greta Edwards, 10 (Atlanta, Georgia)

100 Things to Do during Quarantine

1. Learn a different language.
2. Wash your hands.
3. Put something in the microwave, like cheese, and wait for the exact time it melts, then write it down.
4. Make a play with your family.
5. Start a new hobby.
6. Watch old movies that your parents loved when they were kids.
7. Read awesome books, like my favorite and my cousin's favorite is *Emily Windsnap*. It's about a mermaid and inspired me for one of my poems; it's a great book.
8. FaceTime.
9. Write in your diary.
10. Make a boring song about quarantine.

11. Convince your parents to get you a pet. (It's working for me, it's the perfect time.)
12. Search the web for quarter dances you can learn to your favorite songs.
13. Annoy your brother.
14. Design fashion.
15. Write a speech.
16. Make a poem.
17. Ride your bike.
18. Make smoothies.
19. Make a video.
20. Play with old, old toys.
21. Watch epic fail videos.
22. Make a potion.
23. Make a book.
24. Make a collage. (I have my own collage book, it's very entertaining.)
25. Do yoga.
26. Do exercises.
27. Write your own song.
28. Play tic-tac-toe.
29. Play new Sorry.
30. Clean your room. (Hey, I never said it was FUN things to do in quarantine.)
31. Have a water gun fight.
32. Break out all your old do-it-yourself Christmas presents, like make-your-own bracelet or make-your-own bath bomb.
33. Ride your bike.
34. Take a walk.
35. Wash your hands again.
36. Knit.
37. Crochet.
38. Make a scavenger hunt for your family.
39. Make an escape room for your family. Trust me, these are amazingly fun.
40. Try this on your family members. Walk up close to them and do an impression of them.
41. Do a talent show with your family.

42. Listen to podcasts.
43. Do art.
44. Play basketball.
45. I know you can't do this in quarantine, but this is fun. Go to a different country store (that's not grammar, but whatever) and get random candy. Go home and try them all!
46. If you have a cat, make it do funny dances.
47. Prank your family members.
48. Wash your hands again, again.
49. If your brother is FaceTiming, make him embarrassed.
50. Take your brother's stuff, write a note on it, put it back without him seeing you, and see if he notices.
51. Do a class with your family and put a poster with time and date on it on the fridge.
52. Dissect a dead animal if you want to.
53. Play your old instrument.
54. If your parents ask you to do your homework, make a whole entire essay about science history, whatever, then tell them to flip it over and write that it is completely fake.
55. Make a comedy skit.
56. Do a hand clap, wash your hands right after, again, again, again.
57. Make a bookmark.
58. Use old scraps to make a dress or skirt or shirts or pants.
59. Look at old baby photos of yourself.
60. Paint.
61. Try on your old clothes.
62. Cook.
63. Binge-watch *Stranger Things*.
64. Or if you're too young, watch *Alexa and Katie* on Netflix. It's a pretty good binge watch.
65. Wash your hands again, again, again, again.
66. Come up with your own creature.
67. Make a book of spells.
68. Play charades.
69. If you have a younger sibling, make a video and say it's in the future, and they have to save the world. Watch as they tell everybody to not eat yogurt because it's poison.
70. Plant.

71. Try and learn a new sport if you have the supplies.
72. Make a craft.
73. Try and make a new talent.
74. Practice singing.
75. Practice *Napoleon Dynamite* dancing.
76. That reminds me, ask your parents if you can watch their favorite movies when they were the same age.
77. Wash your hands again, again, again, again, again.
78. If you have Nerf guns, make a dartboard and see how many points you get.
79. Learn to do a bird call.
80. Make a puzzle.
81. Do a puzzle.
82. Write to your pen pal. I have a same-age cousin and it's really fun to have a pen pal.
83. Make a date for your parents.
84. Make a tent and camp out in your backyard.
85. Make a list of trips you want to go on, then throw it away because it's useless, but then all that hard work is gone to waste. Dig it out of the trash, wash your hands. Then notice that the paper is dirty, so wash that, too. Then you just ruined the piece of paper, but it was useless anyway, so you make a new one.
86. Teach your pets to do fun tricks.
87. Do a rap competition.
88. I know some of these are kind of boring, but my mom says that there's going to be younger kids doing this too.
89. Do the splits, but then realize that you can't do the splits. Ask your parents to lift you out of the splits.
90. Do a dance party.
91. Look at cookbooks.
92. Try to make your parents laugh.
93. Do funny things with your brother, like we listen to "Danger Zone" and we would be fun and innocent, but when it says, "danger zone", we would have angry faces. When I do my angry face for "Danger Zone," everybody in my family laughs.
94. Practice juggling.
95. Make a circus.
96. Wash your hands again, again, again, again, again, again.

97. Play a game like Spot It.
98. Do the chicken dance.
99. Come up with your own dance.
100. Make up your own list of things to do with your family in quarantine.

Courtesy of Crystal Bowden, *Clothed Mole Rat Magazine*

Lillian, 13
(Ford Heights, Illinois)

My mom was a nurse and my uncle was a firefighter. They both died of the virus and I have been crying every day for a long time. My father says they liked each other a lot and are keeping each other company in heaven.

Timothy Willinger, 10
(Boulder, Colorado)

I like being home from school because I get to have my big sister help me more with my homework. Before, she didn't do anything much to help me. I think she is afraid I'm going to get the coronavirus, so she is being extra nice. And I am trying to be nice to her too.

Deanna Majors, 10
(Oklahoma City, Oklahoma)

I like that I can be home with my mom and dad because I really love them. Plus, I don't want them to be sick. The only thing bad is that they talk all the time about the coronavirus. Maybe they think I'm not hearing them, but I am, and it makes me more scared when they talk about it. I am scared enough already.

Ryan Slater, 10
(Watch Hill, Rhode Island)

Dear Healthcare Workers,

You must be so scared of catching COVID-19 when you take care of people who are sick with it. I am sorry for you to go to work every day and to leave your families. I hope if you have kids, they are okay.

All my friends are thinking of you. My teacher said everyone in my class should write a letter to you, but I would've done it anyway. You are all very brave and strong, and please keep it up.

I hope there is enough medicine left if you get sick from the virus. Thank you so much for doing what you do.

Love,

Ryan

Lacey, 13
(Covington, Louisiana)

March 12, 2020

Everything was normal. I went to my classes, laughed with my friends, had a great day and went home at the end. No one was concerned about coronavirus then.

Fast forward the next day on the news, I see that school will be closed and everyone will be quarantined. At first, I was mad but then I was worried about how something no one cared about turned into a hot topic in less than a day. "No prom," they said. "No graduation," they said. Of course, the seniors and parents were furious, putting so much work into four years not to have the ceremony they deserved.

Fast forward two months later, the world is still on lockdown. More and more people die of this deadly disease. "Please wear a mask wherever you go." That's what I heard every day. That phrase said so much it became part of some people's daily routine. It's crazy, huh? In just two months so much has changed. So much that wearing a mask is a normal part of everyone's day. It's scary to see so many numbers on the screen that represent lives lost. It's scary to know that I'm a part of something that will go down in history books for generations to come.

Lennon Dye, 12
(Colorado Springs, Colorado)

Harder for the Children

This pandemic that has swept the world has been hard for everyone, but it has had a much different effect on the children. Whether it is being at home all day or not seeing your friends, there is no doubt it's been much harder for the children. This pandemic will always be remembered one way or another.

I have missed my friend, Morgan, from school. He and I were inseparable. Homeschooling was harder than regular school for me because I got distracted way more easily than normal. I went to a tennis camp this summer, which was fun. I wish that my friend, Riley, from tennis camp, was able to make it this year. I had made a T-shirt for him and for me with our tennis nicknames on them. I just recently visited a grocery store for the first time since this started, and it was weird seeing people with masks on. Not seeing my grandparents has also been hard because we usually get to see them every summer. If there was one thing that I would tell anyone who must go through this again, it would be to never lose hope, because once hope's gone, it will seem as though the pandemic will never end.

CHAPTER II

Our Mid-Teen Writers:
Ages 14 to 17

With the mid-teen age group comes a wider worldview, a deeper knowledge of coronavirus, the cancellation of major life events, and emotions associated with these losses and missed opportunities. Consequently, there are many submissions expressing sorrow and anger about the cancellations of graduation ceremonies, celebrations, summer camps, and sporting events, along with the absence of normalcy and communication in one's daily activities. One middle school graduate bemoans lacking a sense of closure, a sixteen-year-old professional actress addresses the mental recovery from a lost job opportunity, and a seventeen-year-old writes a poem lamenting the "unfairness" of this "unprecedented time."

It is no surprise that the largest amount of contributions to the book has come from this age group. I suspect this is partly because of the shock and outrage at having to miss life events that had been greatly anticipated. Under usual circumstances there is much joy in this period of life, as children and their parents celebrate milestone accomplishments. There may be some common questions about the future, such as: *Will I be ready for the next grade? Will I have enough friends? Will I do well enough to get into a good college?*

As the pandemic took hold in all areas of the country, new and more fearful questions were being asked by kids and their families alike, such as: *Will there ever be a graduation and an in-person return to school? Will someone close to me become very ill from the virus? Will*

*summer traveling be possible? Will a child of color be less safe? Will pro-
tests and economic disruptions continue?* These are some of the questions addressed by this chapter's young contributors as they faced
the worrisome life changes brought on by the virus and growing
racial tensions.

Common themes in the writings include deep concern for the
country and the world, drastic changes during the period from March
through July, new attempts at self-examination and rationalization,
and the formation of strong opinions. A sixteen-year-old writes, "the
realization finally set in, 'normal' was to be unseen." An Asian teen
says, "I am now made to feel conscious that I am not 'white enough'",
while an African American writes, "Us black kids don't wake up
feeling black...but many days are spent being made to feel different
and dirty."

Although many of the works in this chapter may be upsetting to
some readers, one cannot help but admire the courage of these writers
in making their feelings and opinions known with such tremendous
clarity. What also astounded me was the level of sophistication in the
written expressions of fourteen- to seventeen-year-old adolescents.
Mature thought processes can be found on page after page. Their
ability to explicitly define the turmoil of our time, and to do so with
a large degree of emotional equilibrium, can make us hopeful for
American youth. The literary capabilities presented in this chapter
are from voices that need to be heard more often.

COMPILERS: AGES 14 TO 17

James Yu, 17
(New York, New York)

Submission 1: June 16, 2020

"When it's really late, nobody should be outside. It'll be safer if you wait a couple of hours," my mom had said. Her statement had surprised me at the time; it was the polar opposite of what she would normally have said, and even what she would have said one or two weeks prior. Despite living in a relatively safe region of the city, my mom would always say something along the lines of, "Be careful late at night. You never know." Then, in the couple weeks preceding the quarantine, both my parents were even more worried for my safety. As Asian Americans, my parents had become worried about hate crimes stemming from the spread of COVID-19, a circumstance most definitely not aided by the irrational and irresponsible actions and words, such as labeling the virus the "China Virus". In fact, this fear caused my parents to blow up on me for coming home late, which had never happened before.

But now, my mom preferred that I go out late, alone, to walk the dog. With less people around, I would be at lower risk. Yet, I still geared up as if I were on the front lines of the pandemic itself. I threw on a hoodie, sweats, and boots, as it was still chilly outside. I changed the filter in my mask before I put it on and then put on two disposable latex gloves before grabbing the leash and putting it on the dog. Then, I took the elevator down, and as I exited the building, I saw the security guard at the door, sitting behind a window with a blue disposable mask on.

When I got outside, it was creepily quiet; never before had I seen the city so still. While it may have been late, I had been out at that time before, yet there had always been people around. This time, there was not a single person in sight, nor any traffic on the usually crowded West End Avenue. I could not even hear a car passing on the nearby highway. I could only hear a slight ringing in my ears. This peace and quiet has stuck with me until now as the most memorable moment throughout the entire three-month quarantine.

Even now, I am surprised by the quietness outside. Now that the quarantine and stay-at-home orders have lifted, and businesses are reopening, there are people about. However, despite people returning to their daily lives, the quietness has continued to linger. Such residual effects are visible from my apartment that overlooks Riverside Park and the pier. While some have ventured outside to enjoy the arrival of summer, more have continued to stay inside. Tonight, there was amazing weather, but there were few people on the pier watching the sunset. And, even now, I still have not left my home to do anything besides walk the dog or take a short stroll.

Submission 2: July 11, 2020

As residents of New York City, the hardest hit city in the United States, my family and I have endured a lot. The city as a whole has been crushed, with many of its biggest industries decimated by the stay-at-home orders and social distancing policies. For example, the restaurant industry has fallen into particularly dire circumstances, as many businesses were forced to close entirely or offer solely takeout/delivery.

Admittedly, my family has it better than most; my father is able to work from home during such a dangerous time, and we have both a supermarket and pharmacy within two blocks of our home. However, in another sense, the current circumstances have had an exaggerated impact on my family. My brother is considered medically high-risk: he is illness-prone and requires medical procedures daily. As such, my family has taken extra precautions and has recently wrestled with what could potentially happen come September and the school year.

Over the past few months, I have barely left my home. My parents have been extra careful and have only permitted me, with few exceptions, to go outside to walk the dog or take an occasional walk. One time, during the height of the pandemic, my mom had me wait to walk the dog. At about two in the morning, I suited up to complete a trivial, everyday task.

In fall 2020, James will be a senior at Stuyvesant High School in lower Manhattan. Having played hockey for twelve years, because of a concussion in 2019, he is now a coach. His primary interests lie in the STEM fields, but he enjoys reading in his spare time. James' mother is Christina Chiu, winner of the James Alan McPherson award for her recent novel, Beauty. She believes that James is a better writer than she is.

Kaleigh Martin, 14
(Key Largo, Florida)

Submission 1: May 29, 2020

I am what you may call an average teenager. I will soon be graduating eighth grade from a small Catholic school in Ft. Lauderdale, Florida. I have attended this school since kindergarten and have been with the same kids for ten years. Outside of school, I am very active in sports. I play both club soccer and club lacrosse. I love playing these sports, but most of all socializing with my teammates. I have my school and sports friends, which keep me very busy.

Everything started going downhill when school gave us a month break because of the coronavirus. All my classmates were excited about it, at first. We all thought that the month was going to be a glimpse of summer vacation. Then everything started to shut down: restaurants, shops, and my sports teams. I went with my family to our vacation house in Key Largo. We would do online school there and then go fishing and boating. It was great, this was the life I wanted: boating, swimming, and sleeping in.

In my final year at this school, I was looking forward to Confirmation for which I had prepared all year, the Passing of the Torch ceremony, the traditional end-of-year spaghetti dinner, the formal dance, and, of course, graduation. Most of all I was looking forward to sharing these and other events with friends I've practically lived with for ten years. It felt like closure, since we are all headed for different high schools next year. I have just wanted to go back to school, back to lacrosse and soccer, back to my social life. The future is unknown and scary for me as I worry about family and friends getting sick. I am missing what I should have had as a graduating middle schooler and wondering what high school will be like under social distancing. I am scared but do not want to show it or let it affect me.

Submission 2: July 9, 2020

I turned fourteen during quarantine and I also graduated during this time. I have missed out on lots of my eighth-grade opportunities, but I enjoyed what happened in the end. For me, online school wasn't a big struggle, but I would have preferred to go back to the classroom. Most of my close friends are going to a different high school and I never got to say a proper goodbye. Thankfully, we were still able to have our end-of-the-year trip to Universal Studios and I got to see all my friends one last time before we all went to different schools.

Coronavirus did not just affect school for me, it also affected my sports. I used to be very athletic but stopped exercising when they were canceled. Since things are reopening, I have been getting private training. I love all the friends I made on my teams and hope to see them again. Although I won't be going back to my old teams because of high school sports, I am still very passionate about my sports.

Summertime isn't what I thought it would be a couple months ago. I wanted to be with my friends and go to the beach most of the time, but now it's much harder to do things like that. I guess getting used to being inside more often can't be hard. Lots of my friends have houses in the Carolinas and are staying there for the summer or going to summer camps. I can find a way to have a good summer while social distancing.

What everyone needs to keep in mind is that when going in public, there is a chance of getting ill and spreading it. Due to the recent outbreak of cases where I live, everything is being shut down again. To me, it should have stayed that way in the first place. I understand that people want to go out, I do too, but we have to wait for this pandemic to pass so we can go back to our normal lives. I believe that everyone can get through this and we can be happy with our friends and family again. We just have to give everything some time.

Kaleigh has attended Catholic elementary school and will enter a Catholic high school in the fall of 2020. She has played travel lacrosse and soccer, which she hopes to continue to do as a high schooler. She lives with a twelve-year-old brother, two dogs, and her parents, who took in Kaleigh's friend who was unable to return home on a full-time basis during the early coronavirus outbreak in Florida. Kaleigh's mom is a professional sports photographer.

Photos courtesy of Laura Shaner Martin.

Lilith Freund, 16
(San Diego, California)

Submission 1: June 14, 2020

You know what I think is funny? That one second you can feel so secure and then one moment later, poof, it disappears. I hadn't really felt that until one minute I'm getting strapped in a harness almost ready to fly, to be in my happy place, and the next minute I'm packing my things from my theater dressing room, never to return. Right before California put over forty million people into quarantine, I was in a show called *Fly* at the La Jolla Playhouse, a well-known regional theater in San Diego. As a local sixteen-year-old professional actress, I was living The Dream; my dream. I was going to the theater every night, being in rehearsals during the day, and not having to go to school. I would wake up in the morning in my warm soft bed having control over my life, my schedule, and my choices of doing what I adore to do rather than being ushered around high school by bells and teachers. Although I did miss my friends, there was this sense of independence I had gained. Being with adults and in a professional environment, I felt a new sense of purpose and pride in what I was doing probably for the first time in my life.

Prior to the day that *Fly* closed, we were told in a staff meeting that the La Jolla Playhouse will most likely not close and we will be able to continue our show. That is why when Danny, a cast member, started reading an email in rehearsal a few days later about how our show was coming to an end, I truly thought he was trying to prank us or tell a really terrible joke. I did not believe it. I did not want to believe it. As Danny continued to read the email, his tone became more and more solemn as his voice went lower and lower, and finally started quivering. I could feel all this independence and strength I had gained during the last three months begin slipping away. As my independence slipped away, the tears started coming; I bawled. I had not cried that hard in a very long time as the salty tears rushed down my face wiping away all the work, and all the hours I had put into manufacturing and creating this show. I came to realize, the show, my show, the best show of my life was over.

I thought about with *Fly* closing, that I would have to return to what I remembered as "normal life"; living in a little box house in the suburbs, surrounded by the same-looking houses with people doing the same thing. Little did I know, the life I believed as normal, would not be the life that I was returning to. I would still be living in a little box house in the suburbs, surrounded by the same-looking houses with people doing the same thing—staying inside, literally 24/7.

Recently, on a drive to my grandparent's house, I passed the theater where I left so much behind. It was and still is a bittersweet feeling. I think of all the fantastic times I had there, all the new friends and memories I had made. Just thinking about it all makes me so happy. Then this looming feeling of melancholy returns, enveloping my body like a wet cloth. At first, it made me sad, thinking I wasn't able to finish what I had begun. Then the anger and resentment towards this horrific virus takes over; why me, why now, how come the best show of my life so far had to be ripped away from me? Then I inhale and exhale, take a step back. I come to understand that although my life was turned on a dime to despair, I am a mere sideshow to the true trauma being inflicted all over the world to people who do not have a little box house in the suburbs, surrounded by the same-looking houses with people during the same thing. This

a terrible virus isn't hurting me, isn't hurting the ones that I love, but is hurting innocent millions around the world.

Submission 2: July 8, 2020

Rainbow

I have always wanted to get out and explore. Yet, for the first time in my life, I have been forced to stay in one place. As I sit six feet away from people, watching the rolling waves and feeling the fierce sun on my face, I, for once, do not have that yearning to run. I have found peace in staying in place and experiencing the beauty I am surrounded by.

Even as a small child, I dreamt of living in The Big Apple, New York City, the "city that never sleeps". I envisioned it as my destination, my future home. As I grew up in sunny San Diego, I have always thought of it as a pit stop on my big adventure to the pot of gold at the end of the rainbow. But quarantine and having to stay in San Diego has really shown me that San Diego is my HOME. That does not mean New York will not be my home one day, it just means that I can have different homes for different stages of my life. I have learned to appreciate each home and stage I am in, instead of always looking to what and where the future might take me next. The pandemic might have taken away the possibility of movement, travel, adventure for the moment. However, it brought light and revealed the beauty of where I am at this time in my life, in a way I had never seen before. I am smiling under my colorful rainbow of today, not waiting for tomorrow's pot of gold somewhere else.

Lilith Freund is a junior at Westview High School. She has been acting professionally since age eight at The Old Globe and La Jolla Playhouse, in addition to other distinguished local theaters. She is passionate about singing and performing. Lilith is a 2019 National Arts Award Winner.

Sophie Witherspoon, 17
(Dallas, Texas)

Submission 1: June 2, 2020

There is something pretty incredible about my community. Personally, I have noticed that COVID has only highlighted how much support, comfort and love our Lake Highlands neighborhood has. Here in Texas we are known for everything being "bigger and better". No shock in the fact that this has proven to be true in recent times. The pandemic has closed our schools, communities, limited our contact to six feet, but it has not taken our hope or our spirit.

Recently a drive-by parade was announced on Facebook to honor the graduates of 2020. This event was heartwarming. It epitomized transforming the sour lemons we had been dealt into sweet lemonade. I watched parents, friends, school staff, and neighbors all get their cars decorated with vibrant balloons, red and white streamers, huge posters all ready to surprise seniors for an outside celebratory graduation.

This virus has taken the end of the best year of their high school careers, the time of true teenage freedom before the next chapter. It is bittersweet to see my senior friends not receive closure from school not ending, and the absence of a real graduation, at this time not all hope is lost. There are still ways that we honor them, and this drive-by parade did just that. It does not make up for what they have lost, but I know that what combats this is the spirit of the people in our community. The spirit and joy in celebration is still alive in the midst of loss. Even though this virus has stopped normal life and times are different, we are still able to connect in multiple ways to make the best out of having to stay in our cars with masks.

It was almost surreal how the experience felt, the seniors all lined up in their caps and gowns, waving as we yelled at the top of our lungs out of our windows with posters. Texas is the place to be in the midst of all this crazy, we still got it, COVID and all.

Submission 2: July 5, 2020

The picture on the following page is an illustration of a piece I drew with oil pastels and construction paper for my Lali (Grandmother) when I was about eight, while staying at her house in Palm Springs for Christmas. I have always viewed art as something so powerful. It is a revealing, truthful, and expressive way of thinking. Art allows you to speak without words, and it allows multiple interpretations.

Back then, the little eight-year-old girl who drew that was not thinking about a deeper meaning; she saw only an abstract face... and she liked it. However, now analyzing it, the connection it has to current events makes perfect sense to the almost eighteen-year-old me.

Perspective. Everything comes down to perspective in life. I look at this face, and I see a split. This divide is literal as well as figurative. I can see with clarity that the left side of the face is uplifted, spirited with a light pink background and heart-shaped eye. The right side is a dark ruby red with a teardrop-shaped eye. When put together, the piece makes perfect sense, the two varying sides of the face equals a whole.

Like this face, there are times in life when we have mixed emotions. Currently, we have been forced to stop our own lives when this pandemic changed everything. Living in Dallas, all of my summer plans were hijacked. First it was spring break, my vacation to LA was canceled, then it was college tours. Just last week I would have been at camp in Missouri volunteering. Everything I had planned and hoped for was canceled. There was no debate, or time for me to process this new reality. It came quickly, and without warning.

Although coronavirus has messed with a lot in my life, I have had a change of perspective. Phone calls with friends, walks around the lake, and movie nights have all been moments that I am thankful for, despite what has been taken from my summer. This is what I do know. We can choose which side of the face we want to have. Do we want to have a vision of a better future and be hopeful, or sit in uncertainty and worry about the world's condition? Coronavirus has been egregious in so many ways, but the thing about perspective is that it changes, maybe this will help to change yours in a positive way. What I know now is that my positive perspective overpowers any fear I have of the future.

Sophie enters her senior year at Lake Highlands High School in fall 2020. As a Texan, she loves her country music and cowboy boots. Her interests include running, reading, and baking. Sophie is a grandchild of the late Bobby Murcer, New York Yankee legend and broadcaster.

Evan Stearns, 14
(Falls Church, Virginia)

The world seems to have started spinning backwards. When I look out the window, everything seems the same, but we can never go back to the life we had before the pandemic. I miss going to school, playing baseball, going to friends' houses, and the summer camps I was signed up to do that I love doing every year.

I started going for long walks with my dad's camera as a way to get exercise and be in nature, which calms me down. I have depression and anxiety, and being in nature always boosts my mood and helps me relax. My nature walks help me feel connected to something I care about: the Earth. I am including some of my photographs with this e-mail. The ones of the empty playgrounds remind me of a post-apocalyptic scenario straight out of a video game. It's fun in a game, but not as much in real life.

I feel like we're going to come out of this experience with a better understanding of the value of human contact. I took it for granted and I miss it. I keep in touch with my friends online, and that's great, but I miss seeing them in person and hanging out together.

With all the protests happening, this has become even more surreal. I never expected anything like this to happen in my lifetime. I'm living through history.

Theo Jacobs, 16 (New York, New York)

Skyscraper

The air used to smell like snow
And cold
And dead leaves
But now it's changed to summertime
And flower buds
And pollen
I watched the leaves unfold,
Watching from the inside

I saw the weeks go flying by
Once March now April, May and June
From thunderstorms to spring rainfall
I watched the leaves unfurl,
Watching from the inside

I put my fingers to the glass
Touched the clouds that drifted past
Felt the sadness of summers past
And whispered to myself
I watched the leaves unwind
Watching from the inside,
Watching from twelve stories high

Katie Weinstock, 15
(Coral Springs, Florida)

In my whole life, I never thought I would be part of such a life-changing moment in history. The coronavirus changed the whole world, and to me, it is astonishing I am experiencing it. I didn't even know what the definition of a pandemic was until I learned about it during my AP Human Geography class this school year before the coronavirus emerged. It is ironic, really.

It is hard as teens, children, and young adults to be in this situation. We cannot see our friends from school, our loved ones, and more. For many, school is their only safe space. This school year, I was a freshman and I was looking forward to experiencing every bit of high school, unfortunately that did not happen. But I remind myself many people have it worse. Especially the seniors. All their work over the years still counts, but it is terrible many of them did not have the proper graduation.

For me personally, many big events and opportunities were canceled. I go to a sleepaway camp every summer and this year was my last summer as a camper, and unfortunately, my last year did not happen. I also volunteer with kids over the summer at my temple's camp, it is a very fun and awarding job and sadly, I could not volunteer this year.

However, one thing I learned throughout all of this is there is always a way to make the most out of every situation. My camp planned virtual sessions over calls basically every week, so we have opportunities to see our friends. Even though it is not the same, it is still heartwarming to join a call and see all your best friends. I have tried to take this time to do things I normally would not do. I have talked to people I have not seen in a while and enhanced relationships. I took up an online summer class to get ahead with my graduation requirements, and I have exercised every day.

One of the most important actions we can take during this time is to communicate. Communicating with loved ones, past friends, and more. Just a simple call or text can really make someone's day right now. It is especially hard for me right now because it is unsafe for me to see my grandma during this time, and I miss her so much. I would do anything to hug her again. I also think we need to abide by the regulations and rules that are placed. It is not hard to wear a mask, to stay six feet apart, and to keep groups in a minimum number of people. It is so sad that people are not understanding the concept of being safe and listening to the rules. It benefits you, your family, and others who you might not even know. My mom, who works in a pediatrician's office, would love to hug and kiss me right now, but she has chosen to limit contact due to her job. If my own mom can refrain herself in hopes of keeping my health up, then you can do the same for simple strangers.

I think most of my generation is really saddened, and upset with the world right now, at least I am. Our leaders were not doing their proper jobs, and the coronavirus could have been handled better if they did. I will not get political, but instead I will say that it was already hard for me to look at the news before the coronavirus, and now it is even worse.

I know this time will go down in history, for the better, and the worse.

Dylan Dye, 14 (Colorado Springs, Colorado)

Stronger

Has it been a year
I can't remember the days
This has caused many tears
Covering everything in a dark haze

People have given up everything
Even I have been in a cocoon
Not seeing friends, family, just waiting
To go to Disney World soon

But a lot has been gained
During this time of isolation
Extra family time has been attained
And a swimming pool as compensation

Wearing a mask isn't all that bad
You protect other people from getting sick
I know masks aren't the best fad
but when wearing it, you can't nose pick

I know life would be better if Corona wasn't here
But it is what it is, so we have to deal
We now live in a world that is full of fear
But we will be stronger when it's over, I feel

Alissa Lake, 14 (Phoenix, Arizona)

Through this pandemic, I realize just how blessed I am to be home-schooled and to have a dad who is self-employed. While everyone else's lives are being turned upside down, large parts of my life are staying normal. I still have school, thanks to being homeschooled, and my dad still works because he is self-employed.

Another amazing thing was watching how our home became a safe and normal place for the neighbor kids to come. While the rest of their lives were completely abnormal, we were able to be a place where they could be normal. There's rarely a day that they're not over at our house hanging out!

All in all, through this pandemic God has brought good things. Our neighbor kids have become more like family than friends, I've really learned a lesson in trusting God through the difficult and con-fusing, and it's really made me realize all the blessings I have.

Maya Tuckman, 14
(Fort Lauderdale, Florida)

All I Know

The world is changing drastically in ways I do not completely understand. Adults say we are living through a part of history, but we cannot predict what the future will bring, just like how I know who I am now but not who I will become. All I know—all that I *can* know—is the heat of my breath on my face under a cloth mask, fogging up my glasses; the whirring of my laptop computer in online classroom sessions, a sea of my classmates' faces, in their homes, in hoodies and pajamas; the sound of my younger brother's laughter and cheers, muffled from his bedroom, which he hardly leaves, as he plays video games with friends he can't see; the gloves and mask that my granny wears when cautiously visiting our house.

I recognize that I am privileged to know these things. There are students whose educations are falling behind because of lack of access to both physical classrooms and digital resources. There are kids whose parents must leave the house every day for work, potentially exposing themselves to the virus, but my parents work from home. There are the homeless, with no shelter to shield them, and those who live alone, with no one to keep them company. And then there are those who work on the front lines, in hospitals. Who are constantly overworked and overstressed. For me, some things have stayed the same. Like the smell of wet grass after the rain, the sound of the singing birds that flit about the trees. But I know other things won't ever be the same. I know I will have to adapt and stay vigilant. So I hang on to the hope that the future will be brighter, even if things don't look the same as they used to.

Ashley Hodge, 15 (Orange, California)

Plague

I had imagined the pandemic would be the end of the world.

I thought we wouldn't see the sun for years. I thought my mom would only dare step out of the house once a month, so we could get groceries. And I thought terror would rule that day.

When Mom would come home, she'd remove her cloth gloves before wiping down the groceries. Then, she'd undress and plop her clothes into the washing machine. Only after drowning her garments in a noxious detergent would she start the load.

I thought I would listen to her footsteps pattering on the tile floor as she made her way to the shower, the place where she'd violently scrub away any trace of the plague. Her skin would scream at every drop of scalding water hitting it.

I thought I'd be terrified to breathe around her once she emerged from the bathroom. I thought my dad wouldn't sleep in the same bed as my mom for a couple weeks, just to be safe. I had imagined the pandemic would be the apocalypse.

But that's not what it is. It's sitting in your bed for hours, as if you are paralyzed. It's panicking before deleting every text you write for your friends.

It's being isolated.

It's listening to your sister scream as your family grows sick of each other. It's wondering if anything is worth it anymore. Feeling your soul slowly crumble.

It hurts. It always hurts. And you wish it would stop, but it doesn't.

Because the end is not in sight. And who knows when it will be?

Lakesha Bellamy, 15
(Lexington, Kentucky)

Presidents Try Their Best

So, you don't agree with his politics. Or you don't like his red ties or his slightly overweight body. Even more aggravating to you is the fact that he was a TV reality show star. I need to remind you that we once had a man in office who was a major movie celebrity in Hollywood. And for sure, we have had other potbelly old guys who wore the wrong ties.

I must confess I'm barely able to tell you the difference between a Republican and a Democrat, but I respect the office of the presidency no matter what. Our pastor says we don't have to agree with someone in order to respect them. It seems to me that for any man to get into the Oval Office he must have earned it in some way. So there, I have said my piece.

Josie Dunnings, 16
(Pine Bluff, Arkansas)

Being Black Again and Again

It's the same thing always. Us black kids don't wake up feeling black, but many days are spent being made to feel different and dirty. What happened to George Floyd was very familiar. In my life it's always been the same thing going on, it's just the faces that change.

At school it comes and goes in waves. Sometimes black and white get along, usually we just tolerate each other. With all the protests lately, I wonder where have all of them been in the past, those same people who are marching now? Maybe they have just woken up to what's been happening forever. To that I say, "It's about time." If I ever used to bring up issues like Black Lives Matter, my few white friends would usually tell me to chill. I never had the guts to tell them back that there's nothing "chill" about being black in America. Is anything really ever going to change? Who knows.

Dom Almeda, 16 (New York, New York)

March 29, 2020

I live on East 101st Street in New York City. Everyone around me is so scared because of the coronavirus or COVID-19. People are walking to the hospital, mostly old folks who are our neighbors, who sometimes we do not see when they come back.

Don't know anyone in my family who has died, but my friends have relatives who did. On my cell, I go to websites where I read about lots of old people who were grandpas and grandmas of somebody. My granny lives with us, she's lived in Harlem all of her life. My stepdad got the virus, and my mom moved into the front room with Granny, so he could be alone in the bed. She passed him food under the door, and he got better in a few weeks. Guess he didn't have a bad case.

Our place is real nasty, it stinks since we are all home eating all day. My little brothers cry at night when I'm trying to sleep in the bed across from them. I wish I could take them to their school. When we wake up in the mornings, sometimes I forget there is no school. It is hard to get any homework done and I am scared my grades are going to go down. But our teachers have been pretty nice about it since we have all been at home. Even though the school building is pretty old and like a dump, I really miss the place.

We usually get Burger King or McDonald's a few times a week. Since the pandemic started in the city, I've been in the kitchen more than my usual. I learned to cook pasta. My brothers tell me it tastes like shit. I shouldn't write like that, but "shit" is how I feel too. So that's it.

Samantha Soderland, 14
(Fort Lauderdale, Florida)

My quarantine life is complicated to say the least! I play multiple sports, and I am also an officer of the National Honors Society. When I heard school was over for the rest of the year I wasn't jumping for joy. I knew that with school ending, that would mean sports were canceled, extra activities were done, eighth grade events were canceled, and I probably wouldn't see some of my classmates for a very long time. I know missing out on the events was harder for others, especially those who have been at the school since they were really young. I guess I am just not that type of person. I also know that not seeing people again was harder on others. Though for me, it wasn't as terrible.

I don't think I'll complain about not wanting to go to a practice anymore. So coronavirus has tweaked my routine, however, what has been hardest for me is the separation from my family. My mom works with adults and children who have addiction problems. My grandparents help out and take care of me a lot. My grandpa is a pulmonologist (lung doctor) who works at multiple hospitals around town. My grandfather didn't stop working in the hospitals and my mom didn't stop working in the centers. This meant that I couldn't stay with my mom or my grandparents, because of the environment of their workspace and patients they see. They thought it would be safer for me because they don't want me to be exposed to the virus.

It still caused me a lot of stress. I am always worried about them, and I miss them. I also wasn't able to stay with my aunt and her family because she has a newborn baby. Thankfully, my very good friend, Kaleigh, let me stay with her and her family. We have been keeping busy by going back and forth from her house in the Keys and her house here in Fort Lauderdale. I will always remember the kindness her family has shown me, and I will be forever grateful to have her as my friend. I honestly could even call her my sister. This virus has made me realize how much I miss doing the things and seeing the people I love.

I definitely feel like coronavirus has had an impact on me physically and mentally. It will be a time in my life that I will never forget. However, I feel it has also somehow brought me closer to those around me. It makes me realize how different my life would be without them. My family situation may be complicated, but I now know that it's a good complicated and I wouldn't change it for the world. I am lucky to have the family and friends I have. They bring out the best version of me, and I miss them more and more every day.

Jacqueline, 14
(Davenport, Iowa)

When our teacher tried to explain what a pandemic was, I really didn't get it. I spoke to my friends on the bus, who also were clueless. That night, my folks started talking about it to me and my twin brother, Jeremy. "Jeez, that sounds weird." That's all I could say that night. I never heard of social distancing. Sometimes I think it's like a game everyone around the world is playing, but I know it isn't.

After a month or more, my brother and I played catch in the backyard. He is a very good baseball player. But his balls are too hard for me. And all he talked about was how he missed his Little League team. Then came April and he missed his tryouts. I can't believe this.

I'm supposed to go to a gymnastics camp this summer. I asked my mom if it was gonna be shut down. She doesn't know. Like, nobody knows anything about anything. I mean it is not like everyone's dumb or something.

Mary, 15
(San Jose, California)

Yeah, it's hard to talk about the pandemic, much less write about it. My aunt was a doctor, who died taking care of people with the virus in a big hospital near our house. She was so much fun and I miss her. She took me shopping for clothes all the time, and then we always went for snow cones after that. No one in the family stopped crying for a very long time. Her name was Maria and I'm Mary. I'll love you forever, Auntie Maria.

Alexis French, 17
(Louisburg, North Carolina)

We had plans
places to be
things to do
people to see
then it all vanished
because of a microscopic bug
a virus
and everything we hoped for
ceased to exist
and for months
we have sat in our homes
watching television
and posting our lamentations
we have fallen to the hurt
succumbed to the agony

of the unfairness of this
"unprecedented time"
yet unbeknownst to us
this hurt is not "unprecedented"
for it has accumulated
and festered for generations
and now it has broken
and unleashed itself worldwide
and we are the victims
of the earth's cruel game
but within our stardust bodies
we possess the power
to radically change our future
to create our own destiny
and come out the other side
stronger, braver, and more alive
than ever

Elke, 14
(Cherry Hill, New Jersey)

When my mom told me about it, I Googled the word "pandemic." I found out that it was all around the world, so I felt better because it wasn't just in our country. At least every country had something in common.

Sofie Brown, 15
(Del Mar, California)

January 1, 2020

The new year started out great. I started making good friends, my GPA was a perfect 4.0, and I was preparing for auditions. My biggest concerns were not getting cast in the play and failing my Japanese test. I had just gotten home, it was 2 a.m. and I was drunk off apple cider and coke. My first real high school party! That's all I thought about, it's kind of like the movies in a way. I threw my worn-out body onto my white, pillow-infested bed and shut my eyes. For the next two months I'd be having the last taste of normal I'd have for a while.

I believe it really began when we got threats of another World War. At first it was a trending hashtag, but then I passed the living room of my friend's house and saw that this was real. The country was scared, and we were all wondering who would be recruited for the draft. Would we go to school? Say goodbye to the people we knew? Was this a joke? But this was only the start.

February 2020

Over the course of February, I opened and closed the show *Pippin*, joined the dive team, and went on a ski trip with some of my closest friends. On the drive back, we stopped to get pizza and acai bowls (acai bowls were a bust, so we all ate pizza). We sang karaoke and reminisced about the weekend we had just spent in the mountains. I never knew that the duration of the drive home would be the last time I'd be with those girls for a while. The world would go into a downward spiral in the next few months. We were put on lockdown on Friday, March 13, 2020.

March 13, 2020

"Two weeks off!" my best friend exclaims as we head down the ramp. "I know, I can't wait for the break," I say, opening the trunk to my mom's small tan car.

"Hopefully we can hang out," she smiles and heads toward the rows of cars and gets lost in the swarm of teen bodies. I hop in the car and pet my loving sidekick (my dog, of course) and turn the radio up.

"You won't be seeing your friends for a while. There's no way this is going on for only two weeks." My mother's expression is blank, she seems worried but is attempting to hide it. She isn't doing a very stellar job, though.

We don't say much on our short ride, just the usual "how's your day"-type talk. The moment I step into our house, the auto-tuned reporter's voice shoots through my ears. The news became more depressing than usual. The Australian wildfires that had been going on for two hundred days were still burning. As beautiful as Aussie is, I was thankful to not be living there. Soon after I thought this, I would quickly regret it.

April 2020

Stuck. I am stuck inside my small apartment with my germaphobe mother. It's like she had hand sanitizers for hands and Lysol for feet. She even went as far as to make homemade wipes for me when I took the dog out.

"There's no reason we shouldn't be at school. Everyone is overreacting." I glare at my mom.

"Sofie, NO. This is very serious. You aren't going anywhere; you could get me sick." She sips from the mug centered on our kitchen table.

"UGH, whatever." I slam my bedroom door closed and lose myself in my latest novel. For weeks, all I did was plow through a five-book series and only got up for food and water. I began cooking and baking a lot, too. I learned how to sew and where to find the best coupon codes for online shoppers. As impressive as these things seem, life was far from normal. We were isolated and unable to touch anyone. In theory, this seemed like a relief, especially for introverted kids. But I liked going out and seeing people, so this task was much harder than it appears. The biggest issue of all was that summer was not very far away. My first summer in high school was supposed to be a blast.

May 2020

We should've been released by now. We should've been able to go out. My Netflix and DragonVale addictions have reached incurable limits. I had a life to live and things to do. I began to wonder, when is it going to be safe? When can I go outside without suffocating myself in an unfashionable face cloth? Social media suddenly became a place of negativity. Killer wasps were spotted in America and black lives were being taken and posted online; posted for people to circulate and talk about. And people talked.

Along with the viral sickness COVID-19, people began peacefully protesting. But that wasn't enough. And that's when riots began breaking out. More reason why I'd be stuck inside watching four seasons of *Riverdale* in about four days. After my separation from the toxic relationship I had with social media, Netflix became my new go-to. I watched numerous documentaries, along with at least ten seasons' worth of Netflix teen dramas.

The word "quarantine" would forever be a PTSD trigger word for my generation. It was scary, it is scary. But it just became harder. We could risk our lives to protest with many others, with fear of getting teargassed, shot with rubber bullets, or just getting the virus we've all been trying to avoid for months. Finally, when things started to let up, shops began closing again, towns were put on mandatory curfew.

So, it looked like my Netflix subscription would be getting renewed after all. Despite the love that Jughead and Betty felt in *Riverdale*, some days it felt like there was no love in our world. The internet began battling over everything, like photos girls posted and quickly deleted because they didn't "read the room". As much as I held lots of sympathy and sorrow for people of color in America, destroying property and breaking into stores affects everyone. It affects the people who put their livelihood into these companies that were robbed. It affects the only reminiscence left of running office buildings being burned to the ground, and it affects the families in neighborhoods where people destroy and cause the National Guard to parade down the street. It hurts me that we are having the same issues we had fifty years ago. Our country hasn't learned that we are all equal. So, on top of all the issues introduced to us over the past few months, we now had to worry about riots. In my small city of San Diego, I never thought I'd worry about not making it home before city curfew. Never thought I'd be unable to go to certain places because my mom was afraid of rioters.

So, I sat in my bed and continued to do the same things I'd been doing for the last three months. But if this wasn't enough, I had to worry about murder hornets and cicadas invading our country, and the serial killer on the loose in Connecticut. So, when does it end? When does the news go back to talking about Black Friday sales and the normal, sinister acts of celebrity scandals and government feuds? When do we get to go outside unafraid of all these fearful things? When does life become normal?

June 2020

Not much has changed. The beaches opened, but for families only. My favorite pizza place was now seating customers inside. But they did start to close early due to riots. I began learning how to sew and sell swimsuits. I also got a callback for the dance team. But still, life was far from normal. Far from what I knew, far from what my friends knew, and far from what my town knew. I learned a lot. I learned to never take even the smallest moments for granted. I learned that putting your mind to something will pay off.

The most important thing I learned is, life goes on. My life will go on and now I will live it to the fullest. I want to travel after high school and start up a swimsuit company. I want to be an actor and I want to be a mother. I had time to finally prioritize my future. I had the time to learn things I never thought I would. I've read books that used to sit and collect dust on my shelves. I watched movies that I used to put off.

So yeah, the world is completely drowning in chaos. But the environment is getting a long overdue vacation. The Himalayas can be seen from India because of the improvement to air pollution. In Albania, pink flamingos are thriving in lagoons on the country's west coastline, where the population has increased by a third to 3,000. The only question I have left is, what are we going to do? How are we going to come together and end this race war once and for all? How are we going to keep our environment healthy? How are we going to do it?

So, you are probably wondering if this pandemic was positive or negative? Was this a positive change or a negative one? People were appreciating the simple act of seeing friends and going shopping. I was appreciating the secret spots on the California bluffs where my friends and I had picnics. That's the cool thing though, nothing is black and white, it is? It's gray. There are people with a possibly fatal illness, riots ruining towns and neighborhoods, there are scary bugs, and WWIII threats. However, amidst the crazy, imperfect world we have, families are coming together, people are coming together. It's ironic that it took being apart to start and bring a nation together.

"Piglet noticed that even though he had a very small heart,
it could hold a rather large amount of gratitude."
—A.A. MILNE, WINNIE THE POOH

Elissa, 14
(Aurora, Colorado)

School during this pandemic has its ups and downs. We have forty-five minutes for every class plus forty minutes of homework for each class. I'm in eighth grade, so we have five classes and it is a lot of work whether you're doing it at home or not. I hope this does not continue like this when I go to high school next year. But I think being in your own house is now harder because it's so weird outside and inside. I mean that everyone seems very nervous in my family and when we go out to the drugstore or the grocery store, no one can talk to you because they have to stand six feet away. So, I cannot wait to get back home. Like it's not bad going to school from the sofa. My mom has been calling me the couch tomato!

Benji Estevan, 14 (Mechanicsville, Georgia)

My dad and I are watching boxing on TV all the time day and night. Sometimes we have seen the match before, but we don't care because there are no sports now. This whole world has this sickness, and I think like in boxing, every country could cool down and stay in their corners.

Abbey Ferguson, 16 (San Dimas, California)

A Teen Living during COVID-19

March 13 was the day we all panicked,
Our one-week spring break turned into three
"See you soon," echoed from all the teachers
But they said it hesitantly,
No student waved goodbye to each other,
Thinking they would be back soon,
Little did we all know,
School would not resume,
Headlines splashed on every TV,
Emails, phone calls, texts,
When everything gets taken away,
What do you have left?
The realization finally set in,
"Normal" was to be unseen,
Now I must be conscious, careful, safe, healthy,
But I just want to be sixteen,

These are the years you never get back,
The only time to be a wild teen,
But these precious teenage moments were ripped away,
Stuck home in quarantine,
Six feet apart at all times,
Even with my closest friends,
Each of us with the same question:
When will this bad dream end?
Physical connection is so important for humans,
That's how love is shown,
But now I can't hug my friends or family,
It makes you feel so alone,
Looking back at it now,
This entire tragedy taught me one thing:
Never take anything for granted,
And be grateful to still be living.

Zoe Rose, 17
(Dallas, Texas)

I've never been a big watcher of television. I mostly stick to movies and books. So, I have really surprised myself with the amount of television I've watched in the past three months. I think I've watched more TV during the pandemic than I had ever watched in my entire life before COVID-19. I've also watched a large amount of movies (nothing new there). However, this newfound bingeing has its consequences as well.

While I'd like to be proud of myself for being so consistent with watching these shows (I typically get bored halfway through one season, which is why I'm so "bad" at watching TV), I can honestly say that it has all been to distract myself from the reality of what's going on. The shows that I watch are so disconnected from our current climate that it provides the perfect escape. Take *American Horror Story (AHS)*. There are nine seasons in total, and each season has a different plot, with different characters, in a different setting, and there is typically a supernatural aspect. It might as well be the opposite of life as we know it. This show provides a perfect escape from a world where we can't get closer than six feet to others, where the problems we're facing can't be solved by magic. Another show I've watched is *The Politician*. Although far less supernatural and fantastical than *AHS,* this show is also wildly unrealistic, thus also providing the perfect escape from reality. The first season tells the story of a high school presidential election, but at a small, private high school in Los Angeles. As a rising senior at a large, public high school in the South, I could hardly relate to any of the characters, but I still became deeply invested in them because their problems were nothing like the ones we are currently experiencing, and I wanted that.

Finding shows like *AHS* and *The Politician* are certainly providing an alternate reality where there is no poor management of a deadly virus, for which I am grateful, but they've also helped me learn that escaping, while great in the moment, is not something to depend on. These are privileges that I have and it's my job to acknowledge them. I'm thankful to have found new time to view more stories that do have good messages, however unrealistic the stories are, but I wouldn't ever want to go through this again.

Rachel Lee, 15
(San Diego, California)

On the Road to Recovery:
Lessons from the Pandemic on Change, Blame, and Inclusivity

Ironically, I think that the pandemic has helped me become more aware of what is going on in the world. As an Asian American living in North San Diego County, the community that I have grown up in has been relatively sheltered. I have never dealt with issues like racism since the people I know are predominantly of Asian descent. Never have any of the people I know personally worried about being spat on or yelled at in public just for being Asian. Even though I haven't personally experienced this kind of racism during the pandemic, I still think that it has impacted the way that I act in public. Now, when I go out in public, I keep my head down and apologize for everything I do, whereas I used to smile at others when we made eye contact. The pandemic has taught me to be grateful for all the little things in life because even the most simple of things can change in an instant.

There is a quote by Leo Tolstoy that reads, "It's too easy to criticize a man when he's out of favor, and to make him shoulder the blame for everybody else's mistakes." I feel that Asian Americans have been made to shoulder the blame for other Asians (who themselves, in turn, are wrongly blamed for the origins of COVID). The point is not who is to blame, but rather the fact that there needs to be blame at all. Especially in a time like this when there is so much turmoil and darkness in the world, we should be focusing on standing together, not standing divided and pointing fingers. The pandemic has highlighted many aspects of the Asian American experience, particularly the idea of belonging (or rather, not belonging) as "real" Americans. In the US, I am now made to feel conscious that I am not "white enough". Yet, when I go to visit family in Hong Kong, I'm "too westernized" and "not Asian enough". The fear that the pandemic has caused has exacerbated these feelings. I think that such acts of racism have always existed in America, and yet when people become frustrated and times become tough, racist actions become more frequent, and racial tensions get thrust into the spotlight. If there's anything my COVID experience has taught me, it's that we all must change the way that we treat others, and hope that others will change too. Things do get better, just never fast enough. Or, as Martin Luther King put it (himself paraphrasing someone before him), "The arc of the moral universe is long, but it bends toward justice."

Jo Kowalski, 16
(Pine Lake, Georgia)

Digital classes
Bereft of perfection
Voices surround me
But there's no connection

The battery's low
Beyond my detection
My computer died
Oh look, my reflection

I look at the time
But not with dejection
My class just got out
The end of subjection

And now I am free
My current election
Is to go outside
No further objections

And here I break free
From the rhyme scheme
And now it is time
To go climb a tree

Yasmin Kerikar, 17 (Brooklyn, New York)

I never wanted something to end so badly. The deaths, the racism against Asian people, being quarantined inside our houses. I never realized how much I took for granted. I am a teenager who spends most of her days inside watching Asian dramas and anime, and now that I have to stay inside, I'm going crazy. I haven't been outside in months. I didn't even get to go out and celebrate my birthday. I want to hang out with my friends, I want us to have our spring break back. I even want school back because remote learning isn't fun. I have never gotten so much homework; I have three assignments per week and a packet every two weeks for my handball class.

I'm up every morning from 9 a.m. for my classes and I don't get off the computer till 10 p.m. or sometimes 2 a.m. My eyes hurt and then I get a headache but what can I do? I have quizzes, exams, projects, papers, etc. I can't just not do my work, that is not like me. I understand that teachers are required to give work, I just wish they realize that every single teacher is giving work now. Not to mention, the AP exams are coming up and teachers are not reducing their workload. I am glad though that they made Friday a makeup day to catch up on all work, even though some teachers do not follow it.

I admit when I was still at school, this was not how I imagined the last few months would be. I don't think anyone truly saw this coming. What I really regret is not going out more and hanging out with my friends. I can't tell you how many times I canceled plans because I wanted to stay home and watch Netflix. But I could do that anytime, I have been doing that every day of this quarantine. Plus, most of my friends are seniors and they're going away to college, so we're not going to get to hang out. Not to mention, I feel so bad for the seniors. It's very likely prom and graduation won't happen, and they have worked so hard (well, some of them have worked so hard) to go up on stage and get their diploma and now they might not even get that.

Our school attempted to honor the seniors by posting their graduation photos around the wall but then most of them flew off because of the wind and now they're under a garbage can. I cannot imagine how they are feeling. Senior year was supposed to be the best year of their high school lives, the final year of truly acting like teenagers before college and responsibilities kick them in the face. I, for one, regret not acting more like a teenager. I want to have those late-night car rides, I want to go to the park at night with my best friend, blast music, and go on the swings. I want to have a memorable junior year because this was supposed to be a year I never forget, and now it always will be, for all of the wrong reasons.

Andrew Lancaster, 14 (Madison, Wisconsin)

Where Are the Superheroes?

What gave Captain America his powers was a super soldier serum. He was called the star-spangled man, but he's no longer around. And you'd think Batman could do something about COVID-19 because they've said the virus originally came from bats! Yet, I think it's probably going to take a villain like Joker to get rid of this vicious coronavirus.

And then there's always Superman to come to the rescue. So where is he when we really need him badly? Well, there's Spiderman who was bitten by a genetically altered spider and that's why he can cling to any surface. Do we think he could cling to the surface of COVID-19 and destroy it? That would be way cool! Also cool is Ironman's suit of armor, too bad everyone in the world doesn't have one of those. The virus could never penetrate it, right? Or maybe the superhero we could use the most is Wolverine, the mutant. After all, he does possess the "healing factor" with his retractable claws.

You could say I read too many comics, and you'd be correct. But I keep thinking about the people who first thought up these super-heroes. Can't they use their imaginations to come up with a cure to coronavirus? For sure, we need a new hero for the world. Or maybe it's time for us common people to be our own superheroes in our own stories. 'Ya think?!

Allison Turner, 16 (Plymouth, Minnesota)

C – O – R – O – N – A – V – I – R – U – S

Careful to stay six feet away from each other
Or else you might catch the terrible virus.
Ready yourself with a mask to wear
Outside when in a crowd of people,
No more than ten in a gathering, please.
And obey local government rules because
Various states have different laws
In these supposedly United States of America.
Riots are bad, peaceful protests are better, so
United we stand, and united we go on.
Survivors we are, survivors we will always be.

Anonymous, 15 (Newark, New Jersey)

My New Video Game

In my head, I've designed a new video game which takes place in a hospital with an interior in different shades of the color red. Masked soldiers are wearing long, bright red doctor coats, and fierce-looking nurses are in red and pink striped uniforms. All have shiny plastic helmets on their heads with tinted visors down to their noses. Their hospital masks are pink, stained with splattered blood of their enemy, the coronavirus.

The enemy virus floats in the air all around; deep red, spiky, fuzzy, oval shaped balls sometimes unattached to each other, at other times massed together. The soldiers use scalpels, medical saws, anything they can pick up from hospital rooms that resembles a weapon. A loud siren blasts throughout the entire game, but no one seems to hear it. Everyone is rushing around, weapons drawn, trying to destroy the red virus.

By the middle of the game, all the floors are covered with a thick red carpet. In combat boots, all the doctor soldiers are stomping on the carpets which become thinner, but slippery. The nurse warriors start to trip and fall to the ground. They are soon covered in red fuzz-balls, some gasp for air, clutching their chests. A red knight carrying a sparkling red sword appears from pink clouds, then descends to earth with his dark red wings. No, he's not like Batman or Superman, and nothing like any superhero ever seen. His sword turns into a large red glittery cross. Whatever red flooring the cross touches turns back to its normal color. Soldiers become regular doctors and nurses again with white coats and hospital uniforms.

Hillary Matthews, 17 (Kansas City, Missouri)

My father is a cop—worst job in the world. I think he is used to not feeling safe and we are used to worrying about him. My mother wants him to be a security guard, which could be safer, but he always tells her we need the salary he makes.

Ever since we were forced to stay away from crowds, and restaurants and stores were closed, Dad said the people in this city would have a tough time putting up with it for too long. No one in Kansas City is very happy. I am busy trying to finish my junior year in high school and the online classes are hard. I do not like it and have to work very hard because someday, I want to go to nursing school. Meanwhile, this COVID-19 is killing so many nurses and doctors—it's a terrible thing. My friends think I am going to chicken out from being a nurse. No way, I say.

Phillip Kellerman, 16 (New York, New York)

Every night at 7:00, everyone in the city has been hanging out the windows, banging on pots and pans. We were laughing the other night because my dad said, "It's okay, half the people in Manhattan don't use their pots and pans, or their ovens."

Valerie, 17 (Tulsa, Oklahoma)

I will go nuts if I can't see my boyfriend for another two months. He only lives three blocks away, but our parents won't let us meet even if we stay six feet apart. Yeah, guess they don't trust us. We are used to walking to school together every day. Then after school, we hang. I'm a good girl. All we have ever done is kiss a lot, but he wants to do more. After this social distance thing is over, I'm gonna do more. It was on the news that having sex does not make you get the virus.

George, 17
(Suwanee, Georgia)

I really started to get worried when I went with Mom to Costco one day after this whole thing first started. We first went to the toilet paper aisle where there was a sign on a rope which said, "Toilet paper back in stock tomorrow." My mother pushed the cart away and I could soon see tears in her eyes. I said, "What's wrong?" She said, "Everything is going to be fine, Georgie." She said it like I was a baby.

We went back the next day and bought two gigantic things of toilet paper, I think forty-eight roles in all, more than she usually buys. We bought more food than usual, too. Me, my sis, and her were not going to starve—that was for sure.

But we had to go back to Costco about a month later for more food. By this time, the town was pretty closed up and we were all pretty scared about the virus. But my mother never liked to talk about it. Neither she nor my father, who got divorced when I was about ten, talk much to each other either. Neither one of them gets the idea I get all the news on my computer or cell phone. My friends and I have talked more about what's going on than my family ever does.

My little sister, who is nine, is pretty freaked, so I try and talk to her. I don't think she gets exactly what is going on, but she is trying to act older these days. The other day, she tells me she doesn't want to grow up, didn't know what to say to that one. Now that we have the pandemic, who knows how long it will last.

As for me, it's like we are on a foreign planet making a *Star Wars* movie. Everything is so different. Now I think I'm forgetting how it used to be. I hope I never forget how much fun my life used to be.

Bob Manners, 16 (Bronx, New York)

BIG BAD B WORDS

It's a Bummer Being in the Bronx
Because now there's no Baseball,
No Basketball, no Block parties.
Plenty of Bums and Bad guys
Blocking the Bodegas, sitting
Butts on Blistering sidewalks,
Boys just hanging, Bored.

My Brother got the COVID-19
But he's Better now.
He used to call me Bobby
But these days I'm called Bob
Because I've Become a Big Bro
And Boy, do I ever Believe
This Bad virus is a Bitch!

Kelly Stanton, 17 (Boston, Massachusetts)

Daydreaming

In the midst of the pandemic, I start to daydream. I have been day-dreaming for a long time before the coronavirus even started, but the time spent alone and away from other people makes my imagination run wild. I like to imagine what my life will be in five or ten years, away from all of this madness.

In this daydream, I live simply. I live in a small house on the edge of a field, near the woods and the mountains. It's just me and the person I love. We take care of all types of animals. There's a cat in the house, and two dogs that run around outside while we work. We leave out sugar water for the hummingbirds and turn our front lawn into a great pollinator garden. Chickens hop around and peck in their little coop.

I imagine myself learning how to use a sewing machine, and making clothes and quilts. I'll hang my fresh laundry out to dry on a clothesline in the sun. I make pasta, jam, and bread from scratch. Outside, we have a large garden full of vegetables and fruit trees. Sometimes there's a hive full of honeybees to get fresh honey from. I get to live sustainably and take care of the Earth I call home.

My life isn't perfect. Maybe the rosebush won't bloom, or all of my teacups will be chipped, but it's my life and I love it all the same.

Why does this life sound so appealing to you? You may be asking. Won't you get awfully lonely out there away from everything? Yes, that's the whole point. Elizabeth von Arnim's *The Solitary Summer* describes a woman having a rejuvenating summer away from everything. She takes walks and takes care of her plants. Most importantly, she lives simply and happily. I want that too. I, too, want to get away from it all.

I'm tired of being indoors all of the time, but I understand why I must do it. Once the virus stops spreading, I want to get away from it all. I'm sick of my own carbon footprint, my own harshness, and the person that I am today. I'm tired of the stringent suburbia that I live in. I know I sound crazy, but I think the minute I get away from the overconsumption, pollution, greed, and instability of the city, I will be happy.

One day, the pandemic will be a distant memory, and we'll all get to live the lives we want to. We'll get there, I promise.

Avery Redlich, 14 (Plantation, Florida)

The Sound That Cannot Be Silenced

Music coursed through my veins.

I heard melodies ringing, lyrics swirling, methodical rhythms beating.

My fingers on the strings, the vibrations of the violin ran through me.

The keys of the piano rose and fell with my emotions as I played.

As I sang—as notes left me—I could feel every word.

Then the world became electronic. While we could speak and learn and study online, we could no longer sing to the same beat. We could no longer play our harmonies and melodies to coincide.

The world changed, and all musicians lost their music.

Silenced.

But some things are too powerful to be silenced.

I felt my fingers dancing along the piano keys, all of my fear and concern and confusion rising to the surface, all laid out across the black and white. Music has power.

While musicians lost their ability to play together, recordings were overlapped and made into masterpieces. Their collective music could not be stopped. Tens of hundreds of instruments now playing together, the notes produced into one moment of time, played days apart. Music has power.

Music infected the electronic world faster than any virus. Concerts and performances were everywhere. For everyone. I belted notes at my computer, singing with the greatest of artists from around the world.

Music has power. Because music can and will bring people together no matter the physical distance. Music provides a strength to those feeling weak, or simply becomes an outlet to feel what words cannot always express or improve. It is a sound that cannot be silenced.

Joseph Mitchum, 16
(Kalamazoo, Michigan)

When are we ever going back to normal? No one seems to be able to answer that question. I watch all the news at night with my family now. My dad keeps saying even the experts are no experts. My mom just sits by the TV, picking at her nails. My brother is twenty-two and thinks he knows everything per usual, and all he talks about is how he's never going to get a job again. My parents tell him to pray, and he reminds them not even the churches are open. Can't believe I actually miss going to church on Sundays.

And so, what about me? I am in eleventh grade and maybe I should pray I get to be a senior in high school next year. If not, that would be a bummer.

Lucy, 16
(Dallas, Texas)

The week Dallas went into lockdown I was actually supposed to be getting on a plane to visit my boyfriend, Simone, in Milan, Italy. I remember feeling hopeless and lost after I found out Italy and the US had both banned entry to one another. Still today, writing this, I'm not sure when we are going to be back together again.

In quarantine, everything is something different yet it is always in some ways the exact same. I wake up, I call Simone, I take my dog outside, I check on our new "freedom garden" where we planted some tomatoes and peppers, I help make breakfast, I clean, I text my friends, I get dressed, I do some sort of work to stay busy (I've started trying to teach myself Italian and attempt, and usually fail, to work out every day), I'll do something with my family, I make lunch, I call Simone, I practice piano, I cook dinner, I call Simone, I watch a movie with my family, and then I go to bed. Every day for over one-hundred days.

For me, the key to surviving this quarantine has been finding ways to stay happy. Obviously, calling Simone is what I spend most of the day doing. We've been dating for a year and a half now, over half of it in long distance. And not just any long distance, seven hours apart long distance. Five-thousand miles long distance. I'd be lying if I said it wasn't hard. Every day we are a bit down about the fact that we should be together. But we find ways to be happy, we text each other photos, we call and talk about our families, we play Trivial Pursuit over FaceTime, and we think about the future where we both live in DC together and have the lives of our dreams. Other than talking to Simo, I spend the rest of the day with my family. Six months ago, I would have hated the idea but quarantine has drawn us closer. We just moved, so we settled into our new home. We've started new traditions like Saturday night steaks, Friday family movie night, family game night where I win every game of Settlers of Catan, and we started to cook every single meal which is something very, very new for us. My days may be a bit tedious, but I've grown used to this routine.

The pandemic hit me hard because having the same routine, however much you enjoy it, gets really boring. Every day now, I'm finding small places to have joy by hanging out with my family, calling my friends, and driving around with my new license. But what is always in my head is when I'll be back with the love of my life. Simone and I have made it this far with phone calls and digital memories, but the one thing I wish for every day is a miracle that would let me get on a plane to see him again. Every time there is a glimmer of hope that maybe I can find a loophole to arrive safely and legally in Italy, it's taken away by some other declaration the country has signed. Like I said, it's really hard. Especially because we don't know when the waiting will end...if it's one week or one month or three months. Every day is another day of calling, laughing, and waiting. But I wouldn't want to go through a pandemic without him, even if we aren't together physically, we are always connected and together in everything we do. Plus, it's pretty cool that our relationship has survived not only long distance but a whole pandemic. So, I'm proud of us, and I know we have the strength to keep waiting and finding things to enjoy and ways to live life fully during a time of such uncertainty.

What I know I'm going to take out of this pandemic is how important it is to find hope and happiness in everything you do. And I've been trying to do it every day. The one thing I have been repeating to myself is this: it is important to enjoy your life no matter what is happening at this current moment. And also, obviously, care about others in the world around you. If people cared about public health more, I would already be in Italy. So whoever is reading this, I hope you remember to be happy and care about other people. :) #wearamask

Elaina, 14
(Memphis, Tennessee)

Isolation nowhere to go.
Schools are closed and streets were emptied a long time ago.
And now my fears have come to pass. I'm alone at last.
These four walls have cut me down chopped me up and let me drown
I'd try to reach you but you've been cut off
The birds still sing and the sun still shines but everything is changing
and memories are fading.
Apocalypse everywhere
It's not safe to breathe the air.
There's a new headline every hour or so...
people dying
Children crying
Pain and suffering
And as I shut everything out
Everyone keeps screaming
So I shut the doors and close the gates hoping my mind won't escape
then I look in the mirror and everything is clearer
I am all alone.
And now my fear has come to pass. I'm finally alone at last.

I grab the wall trying to hold on to something, anything.
Pounding in my chest!
My lungs can't rest!
I'm on the floor. I can't take this anymore, I reach the phone to call
home and no one picks up or hears my fears at last have come to pass.
I'm alone so alone.
I have tried to reach you.
Every day without trying too hard.
These walls have cut us off.
My fear has come to pass.
Alone at last.

Evie Dolan, 16
(New York, New York)

March 11, 2020 was my last day of in-person class in tenth grade. The twelfth was designated a "snow day" and, by the thirteenth, school was moved to online classes. For the next two months, the COVID-19 pandemic was the main topic my family and the world was focused on. We watched Governor Andrew Cuomo give his daily briefings, stayed home venturing out with a mask for groceries every few days, and I struggled to manage the end of sophomore year on Zoom. We were worried about our own health, and the health of people with much higher risk, as well as people everywhere losing their jobs. At the time, it didn't seem like anything in the news could eclipse the crisis of the pandemic. But then on May 25, the whole world saw the coverage on the news of the death of George Floyd at the hands of the police in Minneapolis. Within a few days, it seems that a seismic change in our worldview took place.

My school is known for its progressive values and I had always thought that my education there, plus my growing in New York City, had made me an aware and anti-racist person with a pretty good understanding of systemic racism. But I was wrong. After George

Floyd's death, when I began reading and educating myself on all the injustices in America that I, others, and the education system had overlooked, I felt so ignorant for accepting the way America was and not taking action. It is now so clear that a country built on slavery would lead to entrenched systems of structural racism, and in order to fix it we need to rethink every single system in place.

Now is not the time to be listening to what I have to say about racism, but it is the time to raise BIPOC voices. All I can say is to learn and listen to the people who are experiencing these injustices—not only about police brutality but about all systemic racism, like incarceration and the criminal justice system, environmental racism, voter suppression, and human rights abuses of indigenous people. It is also important to take action and learn about the huge issues facing people all over the world: the humanitarian crises in Yemen and Afghanistan, the fight for democracy in Hong Kong, American fast fashion factories in Bangladesh, Muslim concentration camps in China, rights for the people of Palestine, and over one billion people living in abject poverty. We cannot just accept the way things are. The injustice and poverty and lack of human rights are only this way because of human choices, and change is possible. It is time to stand up and fight for the world. And if you are able to, something that can push us in the direction of change is to go to the voting booths and vote!

(Note: Evie originated the role of Katie, the bass player, in School of Rock *on Broadway.)*

Ronald, 17
(Worcester, Massachusetts)

Most of the time since the pandemic started, I have been following the news on television more than I usually do. I am okay with staying home, except when I begin to think what it is I'm supposed to be staying home for. My friends talk about being bored, and they can't wait to be back at school when this social isolation is over. Not me. I mean, I miss my friends, but I do not miss going to school.

This junior year has been terrible, everyone talking about where they want to go to college after next year. In a way, COVID-19 saved me because I am not even sure I want to go to any college. We live on a farm, which my dad and grandma own, and they need my help, which is fine with me. The cows won't care if I don't go to college. And besides, so far, the cattle have not caught the coronavirus, so I'm safer being with them.

Bonita Castle, 17 (Los Gatos, California)

My friend told me that Bill Gates predicted that the coronavirus was coming. I do not understand how he knew, and certainly do not get why apparently no one listened to him. I know he was the founder of Microsoft, so he must be a real genius. Is it that our country does not listen to smart people? That's pretty dumb!

I live in Silicon Valley, so there are many techies and brilliant people all around the area. I suppose I'm quite ambitious. When I graduate from college, I think I want to be a computer programmer. If I am good enough, getting a job with Microsoft or Google would be my dream. Right now, while this pandemic is happening, I am having nightmares. I hope they end soon.

Manuel Ortega, 16
(New Rochelle, New York)

My family and I have lived in New Rochelle all of my life. Having the pandemic start here in our city over the many places in New York state was a shocker for all of us. The only good thing that's happened as a result was less traffic on North Street, the avenue where our apartment building is.

Usually, when I walk to school in the mornings with my friends, there's so many cars honking and loads of buses, school buses and city buses. This year I sometimes walk home with my little brother, Mateo, who just started high school. We are used to playing a lot of baseball together on the weekends at the park across the street from our building. Now since the virus came the park is empty with very few kids using the diamond. Things are weird; few people on the street, no old people sitting on benches, nobody at the fence watching us play ball.

In the middle of town there are very few taxis or car services because all the stores are closed and boarded up. Not even the candy store where my dad buys his paper and we buy ice cream is open. Life has gotten boring, to stay at home so much can't be good. My mom says things have gotten so quiet in our busy neighborhood that she can hear the birds singing in the trees. She also says she will be happy when the street noises come back. Me too!

Maryellen Roland, 15
(Fort Thomas, Ohio)

What is it like to feel safe? I do not know anymore. It used to feel safe being at home with my family eating a meal or watching TV together.

I do not know anymore. I could always feel safe in a country that could take care of its people. We were supposed to be the land of the free and the home of the brave. I do not know anymore.

When I was a little kid, my folks told me it did not matter what color my skin was. I do not know anymore. I used to think I was comfortable in my own skin. I do not know anymore.

Minju Kim, 15 (San Diego, California)

This Is an American Problem

As a Korean high schooler in San Diego, I didn't experience many changes due to COVID, besides shorter AP tests and a break from school. However, as quarantine progressed and everyone was confined to their homes, the situation became uncomfortable. I heard about racism against Asians and blacks but thought racism was foreign; I hadn't personally experienced it—at least, I hadn't thought I had. But I realized that certain jokes, coming from Asians and other races, showed hints of racial resentment. As the Black Lives Matter movement became larger, social media showed graphics screaming, "All lives cannot matter until BLM!", "ACAB", "Justice for George Floyd". The idea that police would kill someone for trivial reasons—a broken taillight, selling loose cigarettes—was unbelievable. I never thought a person could kneel on another person's neck until he died, regardless of skin color. I knew some of the messy racial history of my adopted country, but I thought racism had abated—or even disappeared—in the times of Rosa Parks and Martin Luther King, Jr. After all, wasn't that what they had fought for? Equality and justice, regardless of skin color? Thinking about this, I soon started realizing that racism was subconscious. The reason that we had learned that Thomas Jefferson was an influential figure—he loved his slaves and cared for them? Racism. The reason we didn't learn about Sally Hemings? Again, racism. And, more prominent present-day, jokes about why Asians were "A"-sians and not "B"-sians (get it?)? Stereotypical racism. Why Asians call other Asians "disgraces" because they're not as smart? Once again, racism, but within the community. I began to wonder if everything we said or heard wasn't colored (sorry!) by race somehow.

I've lived in both Arkansas and San Diego as a second-generation Asian American. In Arkansas, where the population was mostly white, I grew up in my own little group of Korean churchgoers. As a child, I never noticed that I was different from the rest of my schoolmates (who were predominantly white and black); after all, everyone looks unique, so I thought that my black hair and brown eyes were just kind of there, not necessarily a mark of difference. I literally didn't know that I was a different race from my friends, and although there are many more Asian people in San Diego, I wouldn't have learned about different races if I had not been taught to recognize them; instead, I would have thought that there were simply more people who looked like me in San Diego. I hadn't thought of myself as a target of racism, but I realized there were hints of racism in the jokes directed at me, surprisingly more so in San Diego than in Arkansas. I can't say whether it was the culture of the places, or the fact that I was older, or because I was more self-aware (or as a teen, self-conscious), or a combination of the three, but I noticed there was more subtle racism directed at me in San Diego than there had been in Arkansas: "Can you see with those eyes?" "Wow, you got a B and you're Asian." It was a marked change from what I had heard from classmates when I was younger. Interestingly, these jokes were made almost exclusively by other Asians. Once I started grouping myself with other Asians (because there were significantly more in San Diego), I hadn't really noticed that these remarks were racist, because the population "targeting" me was the same race. It took a lot of time away from other people for me to realize this: that just because someone was Asian didn't mean he or she could be racist to other Asians, the same way that just because he or she had a black friend didn't guarantee a right to use racial slurs. Most everyone at school had regarded said remarks as jokes, but there was, and still is, a very fine line between joking and insult.

In a larger sense, though, there was evidence all around social media that Asians and black people around the country were being harassed and killed due to appearance. There's a lot of racists on Facebook—far more than one would think there are in real life. In real life, people usually aren't brave enough to be outwardly racist. Social media has become a mask that distorts—or reveals—people's real-life characteristics. People become bold behind this mask.

We are all familiar with masks in the age of COVID. Metaphorically speaking, the mask was a necessity, a government-mandated item that protected both the wearer and other people. But there are social media "masks", too. Behind a social media account with a vague name, anyone had the capacity to say anything from the shadows. This "incognito" aspect of social media is what has allowed people to be publicly racist without having to face the consequences. Racism makes me so personally mad because taking advantage of good parts of a culture and hating on "suspicious" parts isn't moral. When I see other countries' celebrities posting about the BLM movement and people commenting "Open your wallet", I want to throw my phone across the room. They have no skin in the game; they're not Americans. Racism exists everywhere, but America has a very large problem with it. BLM is more an American problem than anything else. When cops kill black citizens for walking home but take their fashion icons and box braids ("everything but the burden" —taking good parts of the culture while treating the *people* like trash), or when people comment "Corona" on a video of a Korean *mukbang* with exotic seafood but enjoy K-barbeque (again, "love the culture but hate the people"), that is equally an American problem. America was "built on equality" but its roots are tinged with racism. But if this isn't an American problem, what is it?

Mahbuba Sumiya, 17 (Detroit, Michigan)

The ImPeRfEcT Oreo

Every side of the Oreo cookie is PeRfEcT...as it should.
The filling comes in various forms and every bite gives the
PeRfEcT taste...just how everyone expects before taking a bite.
Birthday cake, red velvet, mint chocolate, peanut
butter, or the original Oreo takes everyone to
heaven every time it touches their tongue.
Everything about the Oreo cookie is PeRfEcT, except me.
Every PeRfEcT taste becomes bitter when it sees my shadow.
Every PeRfEcT side becomes uneven when it catches my eye.
Everything around me is just PeRfEcT, but I am disappointed.
I am a disappointment to everyone.
I am neither the child with a gifted talent
or the child with a perfect face.
"You do not try to be PeRfEcT!" the girl
in a white t-shirt commented.
What does it mean to be PeRfEcT?
The PeRfEcT foundation, the PeRfEcT
shoes or the PeRfEcT skin...
Everyone wants me to be PeRfEcT,
But...
I was never made to be PeRfEcT like the Oreo.

Magda Ellington, 15 (Cincinnati, Ohio)

The Mask

These days it is like an awful curse
Not like worn by a doctor or a nurse.
The illness is called coronavirus
A devilish sickness is among us.
Are we protecting ourselves or others?
"Just wear it," say our worried mothers.
A mask looks like we've something to hide,
Maybe it is all the bad feelings inside.

CHAPTER III

Our Young Adult Writers:
Ages 18 to 21

The age group of eighteen- to twenty-one-year-olds represented in this chapter is perhaps the one most directly impacted by the worldwide pandemic. This is, in part, due to the milestone life events that were missed and the future plans that were obliterated or delayed. High school and college graduations were canceled, celebrations with family were denied, job opportunities were put on hold, and known friends contracted the virus.

In the earliest submissions we received, trauma is described in the echoing expressions of shock, disgust, anxiety, and depression. One piece of writing by an eighteen-year-old Maryland high school graduate is titled, "Pomp and Crazy Circumstance: The Soundtrack of My New Life". A 2020 college graduate from South Dakota describes the agony of having, "no future plans...no dreams at all." Another senior, writing in April from a Vermont university, refers to the pandemic's impact on the national healthcare system by declaring, "...it has also proved how our country lacks the basic safety nets."

This age group saw fewer written works submitted compared with the other age groups. Nevertheless, I received many emails from contributors expressing their gratitude for being accepted into a book dedicated to presenting a permanent record of young peoples' voices. Some of the stories were quite long, but I hesitated to edit out the words. It seemed as though these older writers needed, as a catharsis, to express every thought that was on their minds. Much of the writing was deeply emotional. They were sorrowful yet determined, fearful yet hopeful. Contributors and compilers described financial difficulties, racial and socioeconomic disparities, loss of identity, and fear of the unknown.

What many hopeful pieces reveal is an ability to overcome and transform the hardships born from the pandemic. A nineteen-year-old Massachusetts resident says, "When I look back on this moment in my life, I don't think endless days of monotony from quarantine are what will stand out. Instead, I will remember all the Black Lives Matter protests against racism in America and police brutality." A twenty-one-year-old from Kentucky writes, "I tell myself that everything is going to be fine because, well, we have been here before, right? This isn't our first outbreak rodeo. We can get through this. We will get through this. We have to."

Although some young adults have had their dreams shattered, travels restricted, and futures left uncertain, they do have the capability to grow stronger from what has been witnessed. Another twenty-one-year-old, a Georgia native, aptly expresses, "As I look this pandemic in the face and feel all the pain from things it has taken away from me, I struggle to turn it into any good at all. Every day I wake up and try to think about a new life in a new way that makes me feel better. It's like trying on different hats until one feels right, just looking for that perspective that is just right enough to keep me going forward."

And go forward they will. This generation of future leaders will someday dig us out from many disasters and will reestablish the United States as a respected country. This chapter contains the words of louder, more insistent voices who demand to be heard. They are visionaries who will undoubtedly help to make our nation, and the world, a better atmosphere to live in.

Compilers: Ages 18 to 21

Sophia Larson, 19, Assistant Editor (Manchester-by-the-Sea, Massachusetts)

Submission 1: May 8, 2020

Little things let me know I'm hurting. I didn't notice them at first, because at least I'm alive, at least my family is alive. I don't feel any overwhelming grief or fear, but for the first time in my life I woke up angry. I wasn't even fully awake yet, but my jaw was tight and clenched, my neck and back were slick, and I felt like raging against my pillow, and my covers, and the light streaming through my window. I have nothing more to complain about than most, and much less than some, but I've always prided myself on being level-headed, and now that's gone. I spend all day, every day just a little bit angry. I find myself going on a run, or a walk, or a drive to nowhere multiple times in a day to compose myself.

Ever since I was a kid, I've felt anxious about being confined. I've always had anxiety, but the first time I can remember that panicked, tunnel-vision, unbearable kind of anxiety came from feeling trapped. It might have been a shirt that fit too tight, or a cramped elevator, or a room with no AC that would set me off. Over time, I learned to cope, to accept these feelings. Quarantine feels like a coping marathon. I feel as though I'm always on the brink of cracking. I think I have built up a large threshold for anxiety; that I can always feel like I'm on the brink without ever finding it. It could just be an illusion.

My mom is a pediatric nurse. She doesn't work in the emergency room, and she doesn't knowingly deal with people who are sick with COVID-19, but I still worry. People keep leaving flowers and candies on our doorstep as a thank you. The flowers brighten up quarantine a little bit. Something about quarantine makes being home alone feel much more lonely. When she goes to work, I feel powerless and trapped. There's nothing I can do to protect her, except sit and wait. So that's what I do, I sit and I wait.

Submission 2: June 22, 2020

Life, Liberty, and the Pursuit of Happiness

I rest wakefully,
So I sleep restlessly.
Strenuous stagnation.
I used to feel myself moving through life,
Now I feel life moving through me.
A product of a system.
Made in America™,
Made for America™.
I was raised on active shooters and climate change.
On the ashes of the Twin Towers and the deserts of Iraq.
On "Law & Order" and black funerals.
Death was my playmate.
The butt of the joke,
Familiar.
It's a privilege to be a spectator.
Amongst lions and gladiators,
Heretics and emperors.
Yet, far from vindicated.
Far from detached,
And far from protected.
Watching born and bred Americans,
Bleed red, white, and blue.

At the same time as becoming Assistant Editor in May of 2020, Sophia was completing her freshman year at the University of Massachusetts Amherst. She is a member of the Commonwealth Honors College and is pursuing an English and Communications double major with a minor in Spanish. She is a staff member at The Massachusetts Daily Collegian. In high school, she won a Scholastic Art and Writing Award for Flash Fiction and a Scholastic Press Association Award for Arts Writing. Sophia was to attend Oxford University's 2020 Summer Writing Seminar in the UK, which has been rescheduled for 2021.

Sofia Haskel, 18, Chief Compiler (Redondo Beach, California)

Submission 1: May 25, 2020

I stand by my window, half-consciously observing the view of a sloping suburban street named Spencer. The light-blue wooden house with the man working on his car, the tall, ill-fitting trees, my neighbor Bob's disorganized assortment of fruit trees.

It hit me long ago, walking into my childhood bedroom for the first time in months, suitcase in hand. I was plucked out of a life of freedom and pleasure and dumped back into my childhood home in five measly hours by a virus that was slowly killing the world.

College was my first breath of air, the real start of my existence, the dose of life I never knew I needed. Now I am once again numb, all feeling has left my body, and I am only left with fleeting memories that replay constantly once I close my eyes, each time less and less familiar as time goes by.

That night I got in my bed, which felt too large, too comfortable, and too empty. I longed for his warm body holding me through the night, or the soft voices of my roommates that used to lull me to sleep, or the relentless pounding of rain against my window who's beat I learned to love. I held my knees and shuddered as salty tears met my lips. How did I let this happen? How did my autonomy disappear just like that?

It's been two months exactly since that soul-sucking first night at home. Home? No, that's not right. Home was reinvented this past year. Home walked in the Garden District, taking off my shoes to walk through a flooded Willow St., the secret record store above the Boot, the view from the KA rooftop, sunsets by the Mississippi Riverfront, the long, lamp-lit table at Ba Chi. But most of all, it was them. Their contagious laughter, their voices calling for me, them tugging at my hand, us running toward whatever it was together.

Every once in a while, I am plunged back into the euphoric fever dream that was the dark but inviting realm of frat parties, stuffy rooms filled with purple smoke and the ringing of house music, the antagonist of the still, bland life in the bubble I call my bedroom in Redondo Beach.

Sleep's role has changed. At the beginning, it was a constant reminder of my loneliness, endless hours of tossing and turning. Now it is my shelter—a cave where I'm safe from my own loss. The more I'm asleep the more I can fool myself into thinking I'm still at college, enjoying the sweet fruit of life's offerings. I find myself waking up later and later each day, dazed by the afternoon light fighting its way through my curtains, woken up by a sense of utter disappointment in my reality. Falling asleep is a new adventure every night—I lay on my side for hours, clutching my covers and living an imaginary life where I'm back in New Orleans with my friends, or he is here with me here in my room. I do this until I've had enough of this medicine and I drift off to sleep, where my dreams take over my subconscious in a daunting and powerful way, producing the wildest ones to ever dare enter my mind.

Time has lost its linearity, and the days blur together into shapeless repetition. The one thing that does constantly change is memory—it gets more and more lost the more I reach for it. I feel as if my life has gained the fate of the characters in Gabriel García Marquez's *One Hundred Years of Solitude*. The more they are trapped in their town, the more their memories fade, and history is propelled on a circular loop. At this point, to you, it probably seems like I'm rapidly being sucked down into Dante's nine-ring inferno. But that's where you're wrong. So, here are the reasons why I'm going along with this.

I have finally, for the first time in my life, begun to look inward. I constantly ask questions about who I am, what am I when I'm stripped to the bone like this? Without any distractions, I now see everything through a clearer lens. In isolation, I now know who my real, genuine friends are. I can easily separate the people who care about me from those who do not. I have never been able to express myself and my feelings as fluently as I have in the past month or two. Also, I am forced to confront the thing that is mortality. It stares me in the face and follows me around. I actually never stop thinking about life and death, what has meaning and what lacks it, the relationship between the body and the soul, and what it means to be. I think I know—to be is to be right now, and take everything as it comes. Like, standing in the ocean and facing the waves, arms out, letting their forces knock you over but getting back up each time with a new strength to just stand there.

Rebirth. Now I can put my finger on it. A moment to breathe. Reminding me to appreciate all the things I love. When the world decides to give me back all the things I long for, I will not take a single thing for granted. Maybe it will be easier for my parents to let me go, for my little brother to grow with my example. So, I'll take whatever this time has to give me. And when I'm born again, when I regrow my clipped wings, I'll be as ready as I've ever been. When our world stops moving in slow motion, I will have the bravery it takes to place myself in the eye of the beautiful storm that is my life.

Submission 2: June 26, 2020

Summer has taken a breath and then gone quiet. I, a new habitant of my grandparents' house, spend my days in utter peace. I sit in the lamplit cocktail room, the shelves lined with dusty books, and I smile.

For the first time, I am comfortable being alone. I am surrounded by less people than I ever have, and yet I have never felt more warm, more protected, more free. I laugh, dance, and cry without consequence or obligation. Dreams rarely clutter my sleeping mind, and fare mild when I yield to them.

Not long ago, I sat in the leather drivers' seat of the old convertible and drove to Wind and Sea beach—right hand gripping the wheel, and the left dragging out the window, moving involuntarily with the wind's rise and lull. I watched the surfers for hours that day, sitting on a sandy rock. Armed with wetsuits, they effortlessly wove through the crashing waves of icy blue water, almost reaching the shore each time and swimming out again. I focused my gaze on one of them—a tall male who seemed to conquer the relentless waves, slicing through them with his shortboard, body spinning through the air. I felt his passion and grit from where I was sitting, sighing to myself because I knew I was finally as free as him.

Yes—the virus's chains still hold the world by its neck.

But my reality is filled with love.

It is my responsibility to keep them safe from the force decimating the people around us. I go grocery shopping for them, take them for drives, organize socially distanced visits with their friends. And their gift to me is everything.

Every day I admire their fifty-six-year long love story. The way he looks at her, the way she looks at him. It's all I want in life, and the way they share it with me makes me forget the wounds this virus has inflicted on me.

And now, I sit writing this on a chaise in the green backyard, listening to "Une Barque Sur L'océan from Miroirs" by André Laplante, in complete bliss.

Sofia was completing freshman year at Tulane University when she was forced to return home to California. She majors in Political Science and Spanish and minors in Business. She volunteers on a political campaign, manages social media for several businesses, and helps promote diversity on campus. As Chief Compiler, she designed this book's website, ypopbook.com. Growing up with a Colombian mother and an American father has made Sofia appreciate being bi-lingual and bi-cultural, and fostered her love for the cities of New Orleans and Cartagena.

Tess Haskel, 18
(Westport, Connecticut)

Submission 1: June 10, 2020

I would say that being a high school senior right now is very challenging. The class of 2020 has had to face something that is totally unexpected. For the past four years I have gone to boarding school in southern Massachusetts right over the Connecticut border. The thing for me that has been super amazing with this experience is where my friends are from, which is all over the world. My best friend and roommate currently lives in Lagos, Nigeria but has lived in thirteen different countries due to her dad's job, but she is an American citizen which makes her have a really interesting perspective of the world. Without this school, I would have never met her. It makes me so grateful for this experience. But with that comes challenge, that challenge is seeing each other outside of school. Before COVID-19 hit the United States me and my closest friends were strategizing what country we wanted to go to first and when we were going to do it.

When we left, we didn't know we wouldn't be able to come back to campus. So, when I left, I only left with enough clothes for two weeks at home. Living in Connecticut and spending time at our Vermont house during the upcoming break meant that what I left with was mostly cold weather clothes. A week into our spring break we learned that we wouldn't be going back until mid-April and would be starting online on April 1. After that announcement, we learned that we wouldn't come back for the rest of this school year. Since my high school is small, we only have senior prom and not junior prom. I had been waiting four years for these moments.

One afternoon in late March, I was sitting in the basement after I had completed a workout and I was scrolling through Instagram. There was one post of family friends that stood out. They had posted pictures of a home family prom that they were having. I have my prom dress, so why don't we have a family prom? Throughout this quarantine I have been living with eleven family members. On May 8, we had the Haskel family home prom!

We started off the night by going to my aunt and uncle's condo, which is five minutes down the road from my house, for a light and simple dinner. After dinner, we headed back over to my house to have dessert and dancing. My cousin's girlfriend and I had planned the party. We put up fairy lights and bought some disco lights. Overall, I would say that the night was a huge success. This is definitely a prom I will always remember! Even though it was way different from what I thought my prom would be like, it was an awesome night.

The other piece of my senior year that I was really looking forward to was graduation. But my school did not disappoint when our graduation got called off. They sent the entire class a care package. Because our school has students from around the world, we couldn't have a drive-through graduation. Inside of the care package was a Yeti with our school logo, a banner, some stickers, and chocolates. And the most important thing inside of the box was my cap and gown. This was so we could participate in an online graduation and take pictures. On May 23 at 12 p.m., we had our virtual graduation.

After the ceremony, I headed to have a family picnic, and later that night we had a family dinner and a complete day to celebrate all of my accomplishments. Eventually, I hope to be on campus for a real graduation, but with what we had available to us, the virtual graduation was well done.

Submission 2: July 3, 2020

Camp is opening! These are the exact words any camp kid or camp counselor looks forward to hearing in these uncertain times. I am counting down the days until my job as a counselor begins. I have gone to camp since age eleven and always called camp my second home. It is where I went horseback riding every day and hung out with my friends. These were the best summers of my life. I made the best friendships ever that I still have to this day.

This summer I am going to be a lifeguard and teach swimming. This summer there's so many protocols that they have decided to follow prior to coming to camp this summer. One of these protocols is testing.

In many states, there is free COVID testing available for people who aren't showing any type of symptoms. Our directors had to get creative as to how they were gonna go about the testing. Vault Health has a spit test kit that you buy and they email you your results. This is what the camp directors chose to do. Five days before we go, we take the test and then have to self-quarantine. Then, when we get to camp, we show them the results of the test. Once we get to camp, we do it again to make sure that we are all COVID-free. We also have to check our temperature twice a day for the seven days leading up to camp.

Camp has always been a place that is entirely tech-free for the kids and has limited technology usage for the counselors, meaning that we only have service and wi-fi in the staff lounge. With the way school has gone this spring, I think that this is a really good place for everyone to be so we can detox from technology for a little while.

As I sit in the car on my way up to Maine, I look forward to all the memories I am about to create.

Tess completed her senior year of high school at the Berkshire School, a boarding school in Massachusetts, and is headed off to the University of Vermont. She intends to major in Elementary Education and hopes to become a kindergarten teacher. Tess has spent seven years as an alpine ski racer and has been a coxswain on her school's crew team for the past four years.

Nate Bickford, 19
(Lone Pine, California)

Submission 1: May 9, 2020

The definition of what it means to be human may vary between person to person. A large part of what I believe it means to be human lies within the social aspect of our daily lives—especially the small things.

While some are driven to conquer their goals and wear their accomplishments around their necks like jewelry, others simply float. Neither are wrong. Whatever you do, you rarely do it alone—even if you think you do.

Some of the things I miss most are things previously taken for granted—bundling as many of your friends as you can into an old, beat-up, yellow Jeep and driving for hours with no real destination and the radio blasting or sitting shoulder-to-shoulder in a booth at the local diner, laughing and telling stories until we've realized how much time has passed. In essence, the realization that I've come to is that we never truly are alone until we are.

Despite this, the human mind is incredibly adaptive. We eventually learn to find grace in the small things. Recently, I have found solace in the form of adventure, in a time where there is none. For me, joy was to be found in navigating through the old woods behind my house. It initially started as a way to burn through an hour or two on days that passed particularly slowly. Once I found the remnants of a long-forgotten stretch of train tracks, the adventures became less of an occasion, and more of a routine.

Every day, I'd venture a little bit farther. The train tracks became a sanctuary, away from everything else that was happening in the world—even if it was only for an hour or two. I treasured my time there and I learned to find inspiration in a small thing that could be looked at as a simple walk. I found inspiration to paint, and to write—to tell a story.

These things made me feel less alone. Whether it be in a novel or scribbles that you wrote with a pen and paper that are barely legible because you wrote them in pure excitement, writing things down makes it so that whoever reads the story was there the whole time. We really never are truly alone until we are.

Submission 2: July 10, 2020

I caught myself thinking about an old willow tree at a local park that I used to love as a kid. I would go and sit under the tree whenever I needed to think. It offered shade, comfort, and it was always in the same place whenever I needed it, despite any circumstance.

I hadn't visited the spot in a long time. Since I had so much free time during the beginning of the pandemic, I had considered going. About halfway there, I'd remembered they had cut the tree down a few years ago. This made me think about change—whether it is a good or bad thing.

I think about the ways the pandemic has changed my life since it appeared. My first year at university ended in a panic, with people evacuating the dorms like a war had started. Then things settled down at home, and people got used to the idea. Now we hear that classes will be online, at least for the near future.

These past few months have really made us redefine our idea of what is normal. We don't know when things will go back to normal, and I think we're all getting the idea they never will.

A few months ago, we couldn't imagine the basketball season ending. Then came hockey and baseball. Football is next, and then the Olympics. We would only expect to miss sports during the offseason—and this offseason has progressed a lot different than what I'm used to. Little by little, it's starting to seem weird to think about thousands of people crowding into a stadium in the first place. I wonder if we ever will again.

There are other changes. I think people used shopping as an excuse to socialize. It makes me wonder how much of our social lives were geared toward things that meant spending money. Now shopping is a major pain—something you do because you need the basics to live. Small things that we once took for granted really begin to creep up on us and stir up our ideas of what is normal and what is not.

Not seeing friends in the usual places makes us miss them, and it makes us want to go out of our way to spend time and create genuine connections with the people in our lives. We have to make an effort to stay in touch, and the minutes seem to count a lot more. I think we realize more now about how quickly the world can change than we used to. I find when I'm with my friends I talk a lot more about the world and things that matter than I used to.

When I think about the horrible feeling we had when the dorms at school evacuated, I realize something. We, as a society, are even more careful now, because we know more, but we're not afraid. We understand that for most young people, the virus isn't going to be deadly. We're wearing masks and practicing social distancing and being careful and sacrificing for people we don't even know. We're protecting people who are weak, or old, or sick.

It makes me realize that the world can change. All the things that seemed hopeless about the future aren't hopeless at all, because together we can literally change the way the world spins.

People have been talking about racism since before we were born. It is one of the nastier parts of life that a lot of people are forced to deal with, even though nobody should have to. There's been progress, but mostly it's something people accept because there's nothing anyone can do about it. Now the conversations are different. People know that enough is enough, and it's time to change.

Statues that have been up for a hundred years are coming down. The Washington Redskins and the Cleveland Indians are changing names after arguing about it forever, because they know the next generation won't stand for it. We simply will not. New York City is coming together to paint "Black Lives Matter" on the street in front of Trump's building. Seattle is taking back the streets.

There's been some burning and looting, but there's also a lot of joy. You can sense it when you talk to people.

We know now if you can make a whole planet come together, then you can pretty much change the basic things that we do every day. Progress doesn't happen overnight, but it happens. Sometimes it happens a lot faster than you think it will. Change is difficult—it is amazing, mysterious, and sometimes it is confusing. Sometimes things just fall into place, and when they do, you can change anything.

Things are subject to change. The old willow tree isn't where it used to be, and that's okay. Change creates memories, which are beautiful, and it also inspires an opportunity for something new—something better. I don't think there's anything we can't do. The virus has been awful, but I think it might end up being one of the most important events in world history.

Nate is a first-year college student at Queens University in Kingston, Ontario. He enjoys football, writing, painting, acting, and music. Nate hopes to one day have a career that involves writing, and is the son of author Bob Bickford.

Audrey Gabriel, 19
(Peabody, Massachusetts)

Submission 1: June 12, 2020

Arcade lights flashed their tired bulbs, flickering to an indefinite sleep.
Rusted swings sat patiently still on warm spring days, nobody
coming to fill the park with that familiar song of childhood creaks.
Pews collected dust, classrooms fell silent.
The stop light turned green, then red, green,
then red. Nobody came, nobody went.
Empty stadiums. Empty fields. Empty parking lots. Empty shelves.

While the world outside froze like a scratch in a record, we all
held our breath and waited for the music to play again.

Inside was a different story.Inside was a makeshift orchestra—a
house full of kids home from college, a businesswoman realizing
that mornings in her apartment are a delight compared to sitting in
rush hour, a pet rejoicing that their human is no longer a passerby.

The music never stopped playing, it was simply quieter.

Pick up the out-of-tune guitar, play an off-key melody.
You never had the time to learn before.

Bring out the baking pans, forego the stand mixer.
You hand whisk things—it takes longer.

Read. Everything on your list that you've put
off for when you were less busy.
Listen to audiobooks when your eyes get tired.
Write your own story when you grow bored with the plot.

And when the outside world wakes from her rest,
When the fair comes to town again and the families flock to the parks,
When places of worship are filled with choirs of rejoice,
when students take their spots at their desk with refreshed minds,

Remember that it was never just the places that were special.
It was the people within them that made it extraordinary.

Submission 2: July 2, 2020

It happened on the first day of summer. I had just clocked out of a double at the hospital and took my first step outside of its white walls in around seventeen hours. The air was heavy and oppressive, and sunbeams were streaming down on me, drowning me in heat. I all but tore the mask from my face and sat on this old bench in the parking lot. One moment, I was just watching the clouds rolling in the sky, waiting for the air conditioning in my car to do its thing. The next, everything came pouring out of me like a thunderstorm in the middle of August.

I cried. I couldn't stop crying. The flood gates had opened, and I was single handedly watering the parched ground beneath me. I just cried. They weren't pretty coming-of-age movie tears. I sobbed and I sobbed until my skin was blotchy and my hair clung to my neck in some mixture of sweat and tears. My scrubs were damp and I could feel my mascara sticking. I was choking on air and filled the parking lot with the sounds of my hysterics. Coworkers were looking; I carried on with my crying.

I had given little thought to what this year had done to me. I rang in the new year with friends and family, finally happy with where my life was, and thought—this was going to be my year.

For so long, I tried not to be angry. I refused to think about it at all. I powered right through the first months of the lockdown, so busy with remote learning that I didn't have the time to process the events I was living through. Who needs to think about a global pandemic when you've got an organic chemistry exam in two weeks?

Months later, everyone keeps repeating this notion of a "new normal" and I no longer have any schoolwork to distract me from how different this summer is compared to all the rest. When your day isn't packed with classes and meetings that keep you glued to a screen, it's difficult not to dwell on the subject. I couldn't, at that time, afford that luxury. Right as remote learning ended, I jumped into my job at a psychiatric hospital, occupying my time otherwise.

I couldn't mourn the time we all *lost*. I couldn't think about the tumultuous end to my semester or the fact that I hadn't seen my friends in months. I couldn't mourn the fact that I hadn't seen my dad in over two days since our shifts at our respective hospitals never lined up. I couldn't grieve for the hours of sleep that I had lost; clock out at midnight, clock in at five in the morning, rinse and repeat. I couldn't think about any of it. I worried that if I did, I would never be able to close Pandora's box of my woes and self-pity.

This muggy workday, however, had other plans—something in me snapped. Like a string pulled taut, I felt it recoil inside of me and with it, the floodgates broke loose. All because a particularly aggressive patient said to me, "Get her away from me, she's one of *them,* she caused the virus."

(The woes of calling it a Chinese virus. I'm not even Chinese.)

Audrey is a Sophomore at the University of Massachusetts Amherst, pursuing a dual degree in Public Health and Microbiology on a pre-medicine track. After immigrating from the Philippines, Audrey lives with her family in the North Shore of Massachusetts and maintains involvement in her university's Student Government, Asian American Student Association, and the School Based Health Alliance's Youth Advisory Council.

Christina Hohne, 20
(Fort Myers, Florida)

Submission 1: May 10, 2020

My time in quarantine has been quite boring and uneventful. I am in college and we transitioned in mid- to late-March to online learning. Personally, I love online learning. I can move at my own pace and it is mostly focused on individual assignments, which is where I thrive. However, there is a downside to that. I finished all my assignments about three weeks before the end of the semester. Then I had a week in between the spring semester and the first summer session. In a matter of days, my job was shut down.

As someone who works in the hospitality industry at a country club, specifically the fitness facility, it was evident my job would be one of the first to go. It frustrated me when both my school and work got canceled because I enjoy keeping myself busy. Going to those places helped me keep busy. I am a very motivated and driven person, but since the quarantine has begun, most days, I find it hard to make my bed in the morning. I just want to read books all day and play on my Nintendo Switch, which I can't indulge in for too long.

Submission 2: July 10, 2020

Since I have written a couple of months ago, things have been looking up for me personally. My job opened back up, so I was rehired. They have very strict policies and protocols when it comes to the virus. Even if you've been in contact with someone who's been in contact with someone who has it, it's the entire process. My summer classes have started up again and that has given me things to do in regard to my time outside of work. Even though I've been stuck at home when I'm not at my job, I still do things in my own time. I don't find myself having a lot of free time other than that.

On my days off, my boyfriend and I will either catch up on the show we are watching, go hiking, or go to the driving range. The governor of Florida keeps making announcements and new policies as the state opens up more. For all the opening up of businesses that have been opened up there has been a humongous spike in the cases, especially in my area. Even though I've been doing everything that I've been supposed to be doing, like wearing a mask, washing my hands, and social distancing, it makes me paranoid now that so many people are getting it. Things just keep getting worse and it doesn't seem like the government is doing anything about just telling us the exact same thing. Well, we're doing the same things you're telling us to be doing, you opened up the businesses and everything got worse and now everything is going downhill. What did they expect when they started opening places up?

Christina goes to Florida Gulf State University and is passionate about the hospitality industry. In less than two years, she will be graduating with a bachelor's in Science in Resort and Hospitality Management with a concentration in Events Management and a minor in Marketing. She has also been on the Dean's List for the past four semesters and is a part of the Honors College.

Benjamin Katz, 21
(Bethesda, Maryland)

In what was one of the most jarring times of my life, I escaped to *The Michigan Daily*.

The unknown was scary, the world seemingly falling apart. But here we were, all together. We found a semblance of normalcy, solace in the physical space of 420 Maynard Street and the special people, the family we made, within it.

We spent the whole night together in our collective home away from home. And when the sun came up, the University of Michigan president sent the email we had been dreading. We were being sent home.

It was at that moment I realized everything I had looked forward to in my final semester of college was taken away in one fell swoop.

Weeks later, I finished my last lecture of college, turned off Zoom, and logged out for good. Instead of going out to celebrate with friends, I went downstairs, had a glass of milk and a cookie, and went to bed at 9:45.

The unknown remains scary, the world still falling apart. But here I am...

Ben graduated remotely from the University of Michigan in May 2020. During his college years, he was a Senior Editor and sportswriter for The Michigan Daily. As a lifelong writer, Ben felt the importance of using the written word to describe the pandemic, especially from a young person's perspective.

Aidan Ferguson, 19
(San Dimas, California)

"We're leaving Tuesday." I stared at my father in amazement, incredulous that he expected me to get on an airplane and travel across the country only forty-eight hours after reaching the peak of my sickness. He explained his qualms about staying any longer; the entire country may enter a lockdown, grounding all flights for the first time since 9/11. Nobody knew how bad this novel coronavirus was, and because of this mass uncertainty, the nation was beginning to prepare for the worst: a pandemic on a scale not seen since the Spanish Flu.

I had expected to leave UMass Amherst on that Thursday or Friday, allowing me nearly a full week to recover before making the twelve-hour trek back to my home in San Dimas, California. But because of rapidly changing information and the onset of nationwide panic, my father told me that I needed to muster up the strength to make the flight home as soon as possible. A difficult task, perhaps, but not impossible. However, there was one catch; I had to cough, sneeze, or sniffle as little as possible. Just days before, a plane made an emergency landing over Colorado after passengers became hysterical, worrying that one coughing passenger may have the virus. Never had I thought that the difference between a safe trip home and being stuck in Massachusetts or grounded over the Midwest would hinge on *coughing*. Luckily, I refrained from exhibiting symptoms long enough to land at LAX, get in my car, drive home, and promptly sleep for fifteen hours straight.

Three Months Later: June 20, 2020

The world is beginning to reopen. After months of "quarantine" (the word my friends and I use, encompassing strict social distancing, business closures, long days spent at home, and an interruption of normal life), the economy is beginning to open. Restaurants, beaches, gyms, parks, and recreational areas that were boarded up for weeks are blooming into existence once more, albeit with limitations. Hangouts and get-togethers, at one time taken for granted, are a rare treat only allotted to some whose parents are more easygoing. Now that the restrictions imposed by the government have become more lenient, some parents have followed suit. I have a myriad of friends and can see a broad spectrum of the effects the virus has had on different people. One of my best friends has scarcely left her house, and has just begun to see friends, staying outdoors and six feet apart. Yet other friends of mine have made desert and river trips, held kickbacks, and hung out every day.

There is a growing sense of restlessness, a desire to get back to some sort of normalcy that I believe is pushing people past the fear of contracting this virus. But difficult decisions are still being made every day; is the invigorating, forgotten experience of sitting in a restaurant worth the risk? Is the gym, a magnified petri dish, worth joining for fear of getting the virus and spreading it to my at-risk, elderly grandparents? Despite this new normal, it is easy to forget that one month ago, two months ago, everyone was inside, at home, distancing themselves, FaceTiming, attending the infamous "Zoom University", waiting for the day they could return to life as it was before the pandemic. And continue to wait, we will.

Aidan is a sophomore at the University of Massachusetts Amherst majoring in Astronomy and Physics, and minoring in Chemistry. He enjoys working out, playing soccer, ranching, off-roading, mountain biking, shooting, and hanging out with friends and family. Aidan's dream is to both own a small ranch and become an astronaut or, at the very least, work in the space industry.

Janelle Shankman, 20 (Shaker Heights, Ohio)

I fell asleep one night in familiar surroundings and woke up the next morning in an unfamiliar world. A world where kisses are like poison darts instead of cupid's arrows. And hugs have become the enemy of the people.

In this new existence, money, power, and beauty may not mean as much—perhaps that is a good thing. I've thought for a long time that this country's emphasis has been on the wrong values. Well, it's come down to staying healthy, avoiding a dangerous super virus. As children we got over being afraid of monsters, but COVID-19 has regressed us to a place of monstrous fears. Many of my friends are having nightmares, largely absent since childhood. Some are waking up to a new dread of getting through the day.

When we had to leave colleges that had sheltered us, there was at least some relief to being kept safe by homes and families. Yet, in my house at least, no one feels safe anymore. I imagine that parents all over the world are having a tough time convincing children that our earth is still a safe place to be. Climate change was one thing, added to by a pandemic that will surely change how we have to live on this earth.

There are the smaller dangers and the larger ones. There is the lesser risk where every grocery bag brought into the house has contents which should have special care. And every delivery man, mail man, office worker, service person, and anyone you see on the street should be wearing a mask. Not to wear a mask and, in some cases, a pair of gloves, is a bigger risk to everyone. I think the largest risk to our society is in the area of social attachment. Because I am interested in becoming an industrial-organizational psychologist (IO), I have had to take courses in human development. From an early age, facial expression has been an important form of understanding others. And so, when the mouth is covered by a mask while interacting with others, it can influence our communication. When you think about it, the mouth in a smile, or a pout, or a smirk tells us so much about what others are thinking or feeling. With a mask, so much about us, including our emotions, is hidden away. So, let's hope we do not have to wear one for too much longer!

A major question as the summer of 2020 rolls along is, will we ever fully come out into a world that is as we once knew it? Without getting too much more psychological, I ask the following questions about where the pandemic has led us: Will we be able to feel safe in our own communities again? Do those authorities in government or science really know what's going on with this illness? How will our future be impacted by this disaster? The answers to these questions may be tentative and unsure. Yet there's one thing I'm now certain of...us humans are not really masters of the universe; the universe has mastered us.

Jason Dietz, 18
(Boston, Massachusetts)

I was really swamped with schoolwork, even though I wanted to write something for this book. I had little time to write much, but had an idea and spoke to some friends from my summer camp in Maine. I asked them for comments they might have on any aspect of living through social distancing, the world situation, and what was important to them. One guy said, "If you ask me, it shouldn't be called a 'pandemic', it should be called 'pandemonium.'" Another friend complained about the baseball season, saying, "I don't think we're going to make it to Fenway this summer. How can any team play if they haven't gone through spring training?" My best friend, who also goes to a camp in Maine, told me, "The best part of my whole year is going to camp. Think it's ever going to happen? Maybe by August."

I will try to write more comments when I have some free time this summer. Don't worry. I'm on it!

Theo Dolan, 18
(New York, New York)

June 30, 2020

I still don't fully feel like I've graduated high school, even though I got a free dozen Krispy Kreme donuts for that specific accomplishment. Although I didn't get the exact closure that I was expecting, I have spent a lot of this time thinking about the value of my high school experience. I have been spending every night over Zoom playing games and reminiscing with my close friends. And even though we have been apart for the last few months of our lives, I feel like this experience will bring our grade closer together. We certainly won't forget our graduation.

I am certainly sad that this was the way that my high school experience ended, but I am not complaining. There are people dying every day, from coronavirus or police brutality, and it feels like many people have focused on the hardships of the class of 2020. It makes me feel a little weird because what I've had to do is nothing close to the struggles of those facing serious problems. That's why I feel somewhat of a disconnect when Obama gives an address for all high schoolers, to make us feel better for all that we have lost.

The television addresses have made me feel sad, as have many of the celebrations my school or my family have organized to celebrate the class of 2020. I imagine I would be just as sad at an in-person graduation, if not more so because it is such a definitive end to such a big part of all of our lives. While in quarantine, I have been able to ignore the end of high school for almost the entire time. I have been enjoying every individual day in quarantine, learning how to cook and drive, spending a lot of time reading or watching classic movies, so I can avoid the thought that each day I spend in isolation is a day less that I spend with those who a few months ago I saw walking down the halls, or the teachers who have shaped me.

The silver lining for me was the time I got to spend with my family—time that I wouldn't have taken advantage of otherwise. We spent days puzzling, and playing board games, and started watching a family show. This is time that I would not have taken advantage of if there wasn't a global pandemic, and I am very thankful for it because for the next four years I won't be around them all the time.

While the end of high school has been disappointing, there have been many silver linings that I have chosen to spend most of my time focusing on. I have no power to change these circumstances, but I do have the power to control my attitude.

Jessilyn Jeffreys, 20 (Salt Lake City, Utah)

June 14, 2020

An Ordeal Getting Home

Christmas vacation 2019 was fun, and by New Year's Day I was totally excited. On January 5, I was leaving for Madrid, Spain where I was spending my junior year spring semester.

Three friends from college and I met at JFK airport after my early morning flight from Salt Lake City. We had dinner together, all of us so excited to be going abroad. I had barely been beyond Utah except to attend college in Michigan. Our flight to Madrid was uneventful and we landed on time. The Study Abroad representative drove us by van to our school located about five miles from the capitol city.

We started classes on January 12. I chose to take part in English-speaking courses because my Spanish language skills are not very good. But I had high hopes of getting better, so my friends and I tried to speak in Spanish whenever we could. College students from all over the world were studying at our school or others nearby filled with semester abroad participants. In the first six weeks, we had lots of fun. We traveled on some weekends to other countries; I got to see Paris, London, Prague, and Dublin. On the plane ride to London, I met a guy from Barcelona who was at college in Madrid, and we started spending time together when we got back to Spain.

On Valentine's Day, I was with my new boyfriend in a Madrid bar where we watched TV and heard the news that the COVID-19 virus was soon going to be rampant in Spain. When I got back to school that same night, my roommate greeted me with the words, "Well, we can forget about our trip to Rome next week. There's a rumor that all American students are going to be sent home."

It was February 28, if I remember correctly, when we and our parents received word that we were to make arrangements to return to the US. As a "farewell to Spain" gesture, my guy Alejandro got tickets for me and two girlfriends to go to a rock concert in a Madrid theater. It was a large crowd, we were all tipsy, and people were getting sick on the sidewalk as we left the venue. I said a teary goodbye to my first boyfriend ever. He was going home to Barcelona the next day; it was hard to leave him knowing we might never see each other again.

With the same friends who had flown over with me, we left Madrid airport on a flight to JFK on Monday, March 2. We could hardly speak to each other on the plane ride, all of us in tears for most of the flight. I did notice a few people, mostly Asians, who were wearing face masks. One family was having trouble keeping masks on their toddler twins. When we got to New York City, two friends were picked up by their families, one friend was taking a shuttle to Boston, and I caught a flight to Salt Lake. We had all hugged and cried hysterically when saying goodbye. It was unthinkable that we probably wouldn't see each other until fall 2020 for our senior year.

I arrived home, happy to see my family, but eager to do nothing but sleep. For the rest of March, I mainly stayed in my room, halfheartedly working at the online classes. To say I missed college, my friends, Alejandro, Michigan, and Spain is an understatement. By April, I was sleeping on and off through the days, and waking at night with awful dreams. My daily life was back to boredom: no friends, no eating out, no liquor or wine, and prayers at meals, quiet home environment, uncommunicative siblings, and respectful dress code. These things I'd gotten away from at college.

In April, I'd fallen into a deep depression, so a therapist was called. She suggested I write in a journal every day, which I tried to do. Never before in my twenty years had I ever been depressed. My mother told me I had been the happiest and the brightest of her six children. As the oldest girl, I'd always been expected to set an example for my brothers and sisters. Some example I was!

Alejandro and I had texted frequently and did the occasional FaceTime calls throughout March, but less so as the days wore on. Sometime in April, he texted me that he had had the coronavirus, which he suspected he caught in Madrid, possibly at the concert we attended. He also told me of relatives who were very sick, and a grandfather who died in Barcelona. Yet he did not seem to be as depressed as me. And the texts between us got to be fewer and fewer. He had been my first boyfriend ever and I'll never forget the brief, but wonderful time we spent together.

I loved being in Spain. It's a country with so much culture; art, music, architecture, literature, and, of course, the bullfights. Spending time there really broadened my previously narrow life. Don't get me wrong—Salt Lake City was a great place to grow up in. My parents gave me more freedom than most, more than my friends ever had. Thank heavens I still have one more year in Michigan. I hope the future starts looking better by the time I graduate one year from now in June 2021. Yet right now the word "future" has a newly ominous meaning for me. I think for many other college students, too.

It's the end of June as I write this and I'm miraculously feeling much less depressed. I've come to realize that I'm not alone in this topsy-turvy world. There's an economic depression going on everywhere, which I hardly understand. I ask myself...which is worse, the fiscal kind or the mental kind? I know nothing about economics, but as a psych major, I now almost know too much about emotional depression.

I am still filled with anxiety. Having never had an anxiety attack before this year, I'm hoping this kind of trouble doesn't last too much longer. There is no history of mental health problems in my family, so perhaps I will eventually be okay. I believe the return to college will be good for me and everyone else I know. I can't wait to get back to the sorority house I'll be living in. Hopefully, by August the colleges will be able to open their doors to classes and students who've been through rough times.

Writing in a journal on a daily, even weekly, basis became too overwhelming for me. But I'm glad to have read about this book on Instagram and Facebook. So, this is my contribution and I hope it gets published. Writing this piece has given me some relief, or at least a release of some bottled-up thoughts and emotions. Maybe my words here will offer someone else some relief, too. My experiences of the past several months were a bit unusual, but I suspect are hardly rare. Perhaps another college semester abroad participant will be inspired by what I've described, but also inspired to continue to travel, to love our country first, and to not be afraid of broadening one's life.

Edward, 21
(Alexandria, Virginia)

My family has been a political one ever since I can remember. Every night, at the dinner table, my older sister and I were expected to join our parents in discussion of the day's current events. We live close to Washington, DC where my dad is a lawyer and my mom is in public relations.

My father was always a Republican, but mom is a staunch Democrat, so things could get pretty hot in our house. Heated, actually! They continuously argue different sides to so many issues and enjoy doing it. Growing up with them at each other has been both a pain and a challenge for me. But Mom and Dad really get along very well, except in the political arena. Anyway, it has rubbed off on me as I chose political science and journalism as my majors at a DC college, from which I graduated last month. I would like to get a job working for a senator or a congressman, but jobs in Washington are scarce right now.

While I have gone to a few of the protests this summer, my main interest is in the presidential campaigns, and I will probably soon become a volunteer for Biden. He gave a speech at my school last year before he declared himself; my friends and I were unexpectedly impressed. He spoke to us about his thoughts on the possibility of defeating the opposition in a calm and confident manner.

Convincing people to vote for one candidate over the other is possibly not my strongest suit. I am not a particularly verbal person unlike my father, the litigator. Therefore, a desk job or a tech position would probably better serve me and the campaign. Because I enjoy written expression, my eventual goal is to be a speech writer. I was on the editorial staff at my college newspaper in several different positions, all rewarding.

With the United States in such extreme turmoil from the pandemic and racial tensions, there has never been a more interesting time in our political or social history. In our entire history, as a matter of fact. With my background, and as a recent college grad, being even a small part of it all makes sense to me. I have to start someplace, so being a volunteer for a high-visibility political campaign might help kick off my intended career path. I would imagine that most of the campaign will center around virtual communication and television visibility if we can assume that crowd restrictions and social distancing continue for some time. From that point of view, along with other COVID-19 issues, the 2020 election is of primary importance, destined to fill future history books.

I have decided to keep a journal of my activities for the next six months. Who knows? Someday I might use it for a book, as becoming an author is another goal. Always an avid reader, I mostly stick to historical non-fiction and memoirs. Yet I know nothing about the literary world whereas I know a lot about the political world.

The worldwide pandemic has thrown many countries into chaos. The thought that the US has been declining in prestige and may not receive the amount of help needed from our allies is troubling. Whether it is surgical masks, gloves, or respirators we may not have the supplies we require or the facilities to mass-produce such items. With the current rise in the nation's cases and deaths from the virus, the connections are obvious between manufacturing and politics, socioeconomics and science. In the next year, I agree with many experts who suspect upheavals to most of our systems perhaps causing great change to our familiar existence.

To be twenty-one years old at a time of massive change on all fronts is somewhat exciting to me. Being on the front lines of what could be a historical shift in our daily lives is what I am interested in. Since I am merely at the beginning of a career path, it is probably best to keep an open mind. My parents have always cautioned against having a narrow approach to life. Sure, I someday hope to have the nice house, the great kids, the well-paying job. The American dream is still alive and well in me. Yet it's certain we all need to be more realistic than ever. For someone so young, obtaining a worthwhile job may take more time than expected. Right now, I am ready to do anything in order to prepare for everything.

What I fear most during this turbulent summer of 2020 is that America may not be up to the task of overcoming difficulties in dealing with the pandemic. In general, we are not a particularly disciplined people. Is it because we have not developed the adequate social systems? For example, we have become quite lax in our means of caring for others, having lived through generations of a "me first" way of being. Or is it a political system that has not served its citizens well enough? There is certainly enough personal greed at the top of government to deny constituents some basic needs. Or is it a large portion of our population that has grown accustomed to the disparities between rich and poor, young and old, natural born and immigrants? These are massive issues that have few clear-cut answers. For too long, our country has not tended to its own backyard, so too many weeds have taken over.

No one person can possibly have all the answers to all the questions, though many citizens who voted in the 2016 election believed a president alone could solve many issues. It has become doubtful that any leader of any country can do everything for every citizen. Therefore, it would seem ludicrous to expect any government to do a quick turnaround from the consequences of the worldwide pandemic repercussions. As for our nation in general, we are not fond of the expression, "slow and steady wins the race". I believe we would prefer to be a country made up of hares rather than tortoises. Yeah, we like a race, but we are mostly concerned with winning at all costs. And to beat an opponent as fierce as a global pandemic is not a race easily won.

Nishant Jain, 19
(Amherst, Massachusetts)

When news first arrived of coronavirus infections appearing in the United States back in January, I had expected it to be contained easily by the authorities (like how the SARS and Ebola pathogens were in the past), and I believed that it would have little to no impact on our lives. However, as time went by, this prediction of mine turned out to be wrong as I watched with shock the alarming turn of events that happened in our country in such a short time frame. The coronavirus ended up infecting an enormous number of people, from a few hundred Americans back in March to more than two million by mid-June. Not only did this pandemic catch me by complete surprise, but it also forced me to change my lifestyle by cutting down on outdoor activities and staying confined at home for longer periods of time.

During mid-March, when the coronavirus began spreading like wildfire across the United States, I immediately vacated my dorm room and booked a flight to my uncle's house in Dallas. I knew that it would be very unlikely for college to reopen for the remainder of the semester. After arriving in Dallas, I spent the next two weeks self-quarantining in a room to ensure that I had not been infected by the coronavirus. After not falling sick for the next fifteen days, I returned to my normal life. So far, I have enjoyed spending time with my aunt and uncle. We would work together in doing household chores (cooking and cleaning) during the morning, and then I would spend the afternoon working on an online Computer Science internship. Finally, in the evening, we would either take a short walk outside or we would play table tennis and billiards at home. During the weekends, we would spend time watching Netflix movies and creating strawberry-flavored smoothies.

In summary, I have had a great time so far with my aunt and uncle. However, I also wish I could have visited my family back in Mumbai and my cousin who currently lives in Toronto. I just hope this pandemic will get over very soon.

Sophie Katz, 18
(Bethesda, Maryland)

Pomp and Crazy Circumstances: The Soundtrack of My New Life

I should be having my last semester of high school. I should be saying goodbye to the first graders I worked with at the local elementary school. I should be at a concert celebrating my eighteenth birthday. I should be going to prom. I should be taking photos with friends in our new college gear. I should be helping plan our senior prank. I should be in Ann Arbor for my brother's college graduation. I should be at Senior Beach Week. I should be preparing for my internship this summer. I should be getting ready for my graduation celebration where all my family and friends would gather. I should be walking across the stage at DAR Constitution Hall and receiving my diploma.

I've worked for thirteen years for this?

I've been robbed.

Mackenzie Daniels, 21
(Sioux Falls, South Dakota)

July 3, 2020

Right now, it is very difficult for me to write down my thoughts, but I feel like it would be good for me to do. Ordinarily, I am a pretty talkative person. Lately, though, since social isolation became a weird way to live, I have found myself often at a loss for words.

When I first realized I was a college graduate with no future plans, I may have been in a panic. A job in a local restaurant which was promised in March fell apart in May right before graduation. Finishing four years of hard work with no ceremony and no celebration was devastating. And then no job, to boot. I'm still in shock one month later. June was always my favorite month, the end of school and the beginning of summer. This year, it feels like the terrible winter that never ended.

I certainly realize this pandemic has destroyed more lives than what it's done to my little existence. While some of my friends have been able to buckle up, look for jobs, go to protests, I have done nothing but watch TV and stuff my face. I do not even look at social media as much as I used to. That includes texting with friends. I've found that most will not admit how upset they are and how sad they feel.

My best friend who lives next door has a large above-ground swimming pool in her backyard. In past summers, we hung out and enjoyed each other's company. It's now July 4th weekend and she's having a party for some of our college classmates. She apparently told everyone to stay a safe distance apart. As I am writing this, I can hear the group gathering together around the pool. I reluctantly put my bikini on underneath a sundress, but I'm really not in the mood to leave the house. I'll write more tomorrow.

July 4, 2020

This used to be my favorite holiday. Last night's gathering was a disaster and ruined the weekend for me. From the time I walked through the shrubs that divide our properties, I could hear the already boisterous crowd. Julianne, my friend and hostess, was falling over herself with a beer can in one hand and a wine cooler in the other. I knew almost everyone because we had all attended the same community college.

They all greeted me with air hugs, no one wearing masks and little attempt at keeping a safe distance between us. Then, that's the way our town has been throughout this whole thing. Many residents of our community do not believe this virus is for real. Even my dad thinks it could be a hoax. One guy at the party said to me, "Hey, gorgeous, wanna fool around or you scared to catch it from me?" A group of guys, all wearing their red MAGA hats, were slapping each other around. One yelled out, "No more black lives matter, no more protests, you will see—wait 'til November three." Most of the girls laughed, but not —instead, I felt like crying. I'm not into politics or anything, but I have come to see most people in my neighborhood and on my campus as complete jerks.

I left the party and walked around the block to get myself sorted out. Behind each house I could hear the laughter of family get-togethers and see streams of smoke coming from barbecue pits or grills. As I passed the rows of small similar shingled houses, I wondered if everyone thinks the same way as the college guys at the party. Yeah, I know, I live in a largely "red" city and so find it unbelievable that there is so little concern about the well-being of all people during such a health crisis.

As a single child, I'm let in on most of my parents' problems. I know they both are currently worried about their jobs. My dad is a car salesman in a local dealership, who doesn't think people are going to buy new cars or trucks in the next year. Mom works as a cashier at Walmart, who is afraid of being laid off. She says she can probably get me a job as a packer in her store. That's hardly what I went to college for. When I was in high school, I had dreams of becoming an actress. But the drama department was small at my college, so they only did one play per year. Such childish dreams I had; so now I have no dreams at all.

This is getting too depressing to write any more. So, I'll end here. But I'm glad my Communications professor told me about this book, and I can't wait to read it.

Geraldo, 18 (Brooklyn, New York)

Some people keep saying this is like a World War, but in a war, aren't there two sides? Today I hope every country around the world is on the same side. When the pandemic is over, maybe everyone will be on one side together. That would be nice.

Shannon Donaghy, 21 (Elkins Park, Pennsylvania)

Seedling

And I do not know what to do
if the sunlight cannot reach me,
if all the scraggly underbrush
and the towering pines
with their great, fanned bristles
and their roots deep and vicious
have a monopoly on my lot of Sky and Earth;

and I do not know what to do
if the rain is too much and too strong,
if my new, green roots cannot handle the current
and the loose soil all around me
hasn't locked me in place yet,
and it's just too soon, too soon,
and the season just too wet,
if it's just not the right time for my growth here;

and I do not know what to do
if the flames of the forest fire bite at my leaves,
if they finish the pines quickly,
burn the underbrush with glee,
and move on to swallow me, too,
if I was planted too soon
and the other seeds that dropped with haste
when the smoke reached the pinecones
will get all that was meant for me.

The assembly of the orchard didn't prepare me
for timing my growth in the real world,
for flood or drought or fire,

for understanding the days and the way they move,
and I do not know what to do
if I can't ever learn,
if it really comes down to luck,
if I missed my moment, by a moment,
by just a moment.

And worse still:
if there was nothing I could have done differently,
if it was out of my hands,
if every moment is plagued by root rot –
and I do not know what to do.

Jordan Spindel, 19
(New York, New York)

Opinion Columnist, *The Vermont Cynic*, **University of Vermont**

April 2, 2020

COVID-19 is a highly contagious virus. It has been declared a pandemic by the World Health Organization with over 6000,000 cases worldwide as of March 27. This event caused a rare closure of the University of Vermont and a chaotic transition to online learning for the rest of the semester.

When I got back home to New York City on March 15, I knew I would be in for some dramatic changes. I was prepared for it all—social distancing, lack of toilet paper, touching surfaces as little as possible, etc. Having no idea what may happen, I decided that evening to get a haircut at my usual barber in case it closed soon, but I was too tired from travel. The next day, I heard that my barber was exhibiting symptoms of COVID-19.

That's when it hit me how close to home this virus really was. The coronavirus is not an overblown concern. It is a real risk to everyone.

Despite the close call, I continue to live as normal a life as possible. I still go to the grocery stores, take walks in the park, get lunch at bodegas, and try to relax whenever I can. Many others seem to be trying to continue their daily routines too. The streets, while looking as if it was an early weekend morning, still have a decent number of people and vehicles present. The same goes for the parks, which are still very active with bikers and runners.

Still, several settings are abnormally quiet, such as restaurants and bodegas, which have not let people eat within them since March 17. Often, there is nobody inside, and more are closing every day due to the lack of customers. The same can be seen on public transit. I traveled on a crosstown bus one day and it was less than a quarter full, with several passengers wearing face masks. They also recently started roping off the front of the buses to protect the drivers.

The only places that seem to be more busy than normal are supermarkets and some pharmacies, full of shoppers hoarding supplies. However, some have put measures in place to ensure social distancing, such as putting strips of tape on the ground to mark off how far people should be in line.

Despite all the chaos, I am adapting to the new norm, developing new ways to do what I need for my health. This includes seeking out overlooked bodegas that sometimes have scarce supplies or going to the park to get a break from studying.

Many are trying to find new ways to keep positive energy as well. For example, every night at 7 p.m., since March 27, thousands of people cheer and clap for all of the essential workers, enveloping the city in a veil of hope.

Despite the proof that it is possible to adjust to these changes, life in the city will continue to shift in the coming days and weeks. I'm afraid of what effect these could have on my life as well as the possibility of contracting COVID-19.

For now, I'm just going to take it day by day, living in the moment, and suggest we all do the same.

Phoebe Nassar, 21
(Richmond, Virginia)

June 29, 2020

"Don't forget your mask!" I hear my mom say every morning as I rush out the door to make my grocery store shift on time. With hiring freezes happening across the country, it seemed like working in a grocery store was one of the few options I had. When everything began closing, it was daunting to leave my house at all, for fear of coming in contact with a virus that health experts knew little about. The past few months have been surreal, considering my college career ended with remote classes and a stay-at-home order. Unfortunately, the pandemic complicated my graduation and post-graduation plans, so I will not officially graduate until December. Needless to say, students, professors, and university administration staff were not prepared to handle such an unprecedented situation. Until now, I never imagined I would experience an event that will find its way into the history books, especially not a global pandemic.

Throughout my childhood, social justice was a topic I felt strongly about. I took an interest in educating myself on the disparities between demographics and volunteered at non-profits to further expand on that knowledge. As I matured, I realized that a significant way of making a difference would be to implement policies that close the gap between those who have a voice and those who do not.

As a Political Science student, it has been an interesting, but overwhelming, experience to attempt to immerse myself within the political field at this time. In the fall, I enrolled in an international health course, which in hindsight, allowed me to grasp the seriousness of this public health crisis. The international health course motivated me to passionately pursue a career in health policy that would involve implementing healthcare reform. Watching our nation's leaders scramble to come up with numerous solutions has prompted me to wonder what I would do in that position, since this is the career I am pursuing, after all.

From a political perspective, this pandemic has shed light on how fragile the American political system is, specifically the healthcare system. The necessary steps we, as a nation, took to combat this virus has proven that we are able to be more flexible when it comes to accommodating individuals with different needs. Unfortunately, it has also proven how our country lacks basic safety nets. The disparities that were obvious before have only been exacerbated by this crisis. Prior to the current public health crisis, I knew I wanted to make a difference on a larger scale. I dedicated my time to learning about the political process, successful political leaders, and American ideologies. Although recent events have been overwhelming and exhausting for citizens across the nation, it has only confirmed my career goals and my desire to make institutional change within the American government. As an aspiring politician, my experience with this pandemic has ultimately clarified the path that I have been hesitant to take.

Nicholas Patrone, 20 (Portland, Oregon)

June 5, 2020

I PROTEST!

I protest therefore I am.
I protest that all lives matter—
black, yellow, white, and brown.
I protest in a free country
where we are free to be me, you, and them.
I protest all the crimes in a place
that's supposed to be for all the people.
I protest so much unnecessary violence

In a country that only wants peace.
I protest that our rights are ignored
by those who have too many already.
I protest for poor people who have little
Except for the love they can gather.
I protest for the old and disabled
Who cannot walk on feeble legs.
I protest for minds that will not reason
For reasons very hard to fathom.
I protest to be told I should not protest
When it's our history to march for a cause.
I protest a virus that as yet has no cure,
A disaster for a world so chaotic.
I protest a future that appears to be bleak
When some hope is needed more than ever.
I protest therefore I will be.

Anonymous, 19 (Long Island, New York)

Last year, when I was applying to colleges, I had wanted to go farther away from home. I didn't get into my first-choice schools and I was mad. Instead, I went to a school in Connecticut, which is less than two hours from my house in Long Island. Now, with all that's happened since, I am so glad it's the way it turned out. Actually, I liked the place from the start and my roommate, Steph, from Minnesota, was great. Sometime in November 2019, we planned a trip to Florida for spring break.

We did not know so much about the virus in late February, so our parents saw no problem with us going to Fort Lauderdale. Neither one of us had ever been there. We had a great time, went to the beach every day and to the bars in South Beach or Miami at night. And such cute guys from all over! No one talked of any pandemic coming. One old drunk dude on a street corner did scream, "You're all doomed!" Of course, I didn't think much of that as a New Yorker. I mean, really?

We got on the plane to LaGuardia and saw a mother and kid wearing masks—weird, we thought. At the airport, no more masks. I think that day was March 8, we got back to college, hadn't heard or seen any news for a week. By Saint Patrick's Day, Steph and I, and a few other girls who had been to South Beach with us, had felt nauseous and dizzy. We joked that we must still be hungover from drinking more than we'd ever had in Florida.

For so many days, the TV news was filled with stories and pictures of "crazy spring breakers" crowded onto the Florida beaches. I was more than a little worried when my parents called to say if I did not feel better in a few days, I should come home. Didn't want to let on how badly I felt.

On March 19, a few of us, Steph included, felt worse and made plans to leave school. Our parents texted every ten minutes on the ride to JFK airport, where Steph was catching a plane for St. Paul, Minnesota. Before saying goodbye, I thought maybe we wouldn't see each other for a long time. There were rumors most colleges were to be closed. When I drove into the driveway of our house about twenty minutes later, I dissolved into tears.

For some two weeks, my parents never asked about my week in Florida. I thankfully had a mild case of coronavirus, although it left me too exhausted to do all my online classes until the second week of April. But then I played catch-up and was able to take exams April 27-30. Well, I made it through freshman year. And just like that, it was over.

A few friends—my relatives wouldn't dare ask—have wanted to know if I regret going to Florida. No point trying to lay a guilt trip on me! Maybe if we had to do it all over again, some of us might not have gone. But then I've thought that many would have eventually gotten COVID-19 anyway. Guess there are reasons, good and bad, why none of us will ever forget spring break 2020.

Alexander, 20
(Spokane, Washington)

OMG—now every ad on TV, Instagram, even Facebook is about the coronavirus. It's a bummer. Bad enough we have to live through it. Give me a break. Yeah, it's awful, alright. I mean it—we need a break. I've got nothing more to say.

Erica Guan, 19
(Needham, Massachusetts)

At the age of five, I was dropped off at my first day of kindergarten without knowing a word of English. I spent my very first day of school bawling my eyes out in my teacher's lap, out of frustration and fear. As a child of two Chinese immigrants, I grew up juggling my two identities and cultures. In my early childhood, I struggled to assimilate myself in American culture and was uncomfortable with being different. I grew up blocking out my classmates' remarks about my small eyes, flat face, and eating dogs. I ignored strangers calling me "ling-ling" and asking me where I'm really from. Now, fourteen years later, it gets harder to simply ignore the ignorant and the hateful. We are blamed for the "Chinese virus". We quarantine in fear of contracting COVID-19. We quarantine in fear of being spit on, yelled at, and beaten up.

Sandy Freedenberg, 20 (New York, New York)

I had a strange dream. I was in my doctor's office and I had an umbrella with me. When I walked out, I went to my favorite jewelry store on Lexington Avenue. It was weird, but miraculously, the stores had just been opened so I went to call my mother from a street payphone to come join me for some shopping. In reality, every store on that avenue had been boarded up for several weeks and most of the phone booths have been removed.

When I walked back to the jewelry store, the sun was out in the dream, but my one umbrella had turned into two. I got to the store and realized that it had turned into a construction site. The store was being rebuilt. I lost both umbrellas in the rubble and asked a construction worker if he had found two umbrellas. He looked at me as if I was crazy, and the dream ended there. Now I think this dream means I really am going crazy!

Meredith Wolf, 19 (Essex, Massachusetts)

Coronavirus came as such a surprise. We knew about it for months, made jokes about it for months, didn't take it seriously for months, but I never guessed that it would change everyday life so drastically. It felt like one day I was studying on the quad in college and watching *The Bachelor* with my friends, and the next day we were being told we had to pack up our dorm rooms, go home, and take our classes online. I had spent so much time planning my spring and summer, and all of that was useless in an instant. Instead, I had to leave all my new friends and my boyfriend and move back in with my family. That being said, I feel guilty complaining, or even feeling sad, about the effects coronavirus has had on my life. I know so many people are dealing with much worse impacts of coronavirus, so it feels petty to be upset that I am missing out on part of college.

Further, coronavirus hasn't been completely negative. It feels awful to not be able to see my boyfriend, but we've gotten closer emotionally and better at communicating. I miss my friends, but I can spend time with my pets again. I am bored from all my free time, but I started working out more and eating healthier.

Finally, when I look back at this moment in my life, I don't think endless days of monotony from quarantine are what will stand out. Instead, I will remember all the Black Lives Matter protests against racism in America and police brutality in particular. I've always agreed with the Black Lives Matter movement, but this moment in time showed me I need to be more active. It has caused me to think deeper about issues in my predominantly white communities (both my hometown and my college) and realize just how much progress needs to be made. I hope to spend the rest of quarantine learning more and educating myself, and hopefully helping to fight against some of these issues.

William Landsman, 21
(Washington, Connecticut)

June 23, 2020

It used to be that the tone of everyday America was what allowed us to survive. For instance, the encounters with friends, talking with our families, anticipation of special events, visits with our relatives, hanging together at a movie or a restaurant. These once common occurrences are a good part of the loss we all feel since the pandemic began.

I suspect that now men, women, children are all consumed with not knowing if we will ever get back to life as we knew it. My grandpa says, "This too will pass," and my parents tell me, "We have to be brave in order to get past this." My friends, trying to enjoy themselves in the summer of 2020, nevertheless complain about the activities they miss, like parties, team sports, drunken nights. They longingly remember sneaking into bars, walking beaches to look at bikini-clad girls, drives to the city, and going to movies in gangs.

Us guys have grown up believing men are the strong sex. At twenty-one, we are on the cusp yet these days feel far from manly. Like in baseball, big guys don't cry—NOT! In the last few months, I've seen plenty of tears in my dad's eyes, mostly when he's been talking about job insecurity or the government's handling of the pandemic. Some nights, I cry a little out of self-pity, the sadness of young years over too soon. I cry too for a future of uncertainty, a college career so quickly struck by the lightning bolt of the coronavirus pandemic. In a flash, I felt myself as if lying flat on the ground, not knowing how or if I could stand up.

Not quite believing it, I actually am now convinced that women are really the stronger sex. Ever since we are all home together so much, I've watched my mother more closely. She cooks meals with a limited supply of food, never complaining and often creating dishes that our family has never seen before. She jokingly refers to dinners as "potluck—too bad you don't like." Whereas she had little sense of humor before the pandemic, she's now the lighter, assertive leader of our tribe. Mealtimes have turned into fun events with the five of us sitting in comfort, enjoying each other's company. We used to gobble up food in order to get up from the table as soon as possible with my dad yelling at us about rushing off. He is still pretty solemn, but Mom is holding us together. Her wit, good nature, and inner strength facing near calamity are admirable.

My fourteen-year-old sister has a lot of our mom in her. She has become more cheerful given what's going on, and I know she's scared. She has never been into sports much, yet she has been willing to do hoops with him on the garage door net. She jokes about how her shots are so awful, allowing Jon, who's twelve, to tease her. Beth used to be a crybaby but seems to have gotten over it since being in quarantine. She used to squawk about helping in the kitchen, doing dishes, and all; now she's stopped complaining and even offers to help me take out the garbage.

When I go out at night alone to put the plastic bags in our bin, I sometimes look up at the stars, which are bright in our rural part of Connecticut. Our family has never been very religious. We go to church only on holidays. Lately, on some nights I find myself praying to the stars, not knowing if there's a God up there or not. Mostly I say out loud, "Hey, stars, if there's a heaven up there, please help this world down here." Or sometimes I think if there's a force behind those bright lights, it needs to do something to save this planet. I've never told anyone about this.

I believe everyone must wonder if we're going to be saved from this terrible pandemic. People my age don't like to show their emotions. Guess we're afraid of becoming wimps! Maybe the next generation will become braver after going through all this. I watch my ten-year-old brother and question if he's going to remember everything I will. He seems oblivious at times, becomes very quiet when we're all watching the news on TV. Maybe he just doesn't know what to think. He rarely asks any questions about anything that's going on. Yet, he's fairly smart. In a way, I hope he grows up not realizing how bad the situation was. For him, life will eventually go back to some kind of normal so his teen years might be okay.

Who knows what kind of life lies ahead for anyone anymore? Hey, I just thought of something—Gen Z, "Z" is at the end of the alphabet. Maybe that means we all get to start all over again.

Liliana Krug, 18
(New York, New York)

Safe. Safety. Safe places. What makes a place safe or unsafe? I live in New York City. The city that never sleeps. A place where I have been told to "be careful" by adults around me since I started walking around by myself. But I rarely, if ever, felt truly unsafe. Even if it was late at night and I was on the subway, there were always people. People on the streets of my neighborhood at 1:00 a.m. and people in the subways I took home late at midnight. Of course, there were times when I felt unsafe for a moment. Creepy people are to blame, but that isn't all about the time of day. There are people who unsettled me in the subway and people who alarmed me on the streets. More of these figures emerge as the sun sets, but I still would say that I felt pretty safe in New York City. Yet, in one day that fully changed.

I remember getting on the subway to go to school the morning of Friday, March 13. I got on the same subway I had ridden throughout all of high school, hoping to find a seat for my thirteen-stop commute to school. The train doors opened—the third car of the train—and it looked the same way it did at midnight on a Friday night. There were people, but not as many as I was used to. I was used to the train being so crowded I had to politely push my way into the car, removing and holding my backpack by my feet. I was used to bodies, so many bodies that you could barely breathe. If this were any other day and I was lucky, there would be one seat open that I may or may not get but there would be a pole for me to hold. That was not a guarantee.

On the morning of Friday March 13, there were so many seats open because no one was sitting directly next to each other. I made a quick decision to move to the side of the subway car instead of going for a seat in the middle of the car. I figured there were less people I would come in contact with this way. I took the seat next to the door so, at most, I would only have one person sitting next to me because on my other side was a pole. I didn't touch this pole or lean against it as I had done many times before, resting my tired head against the cold metal. I didn't touch anything, in fact. I just put my backpack on my lap and sat there. I didn't take out my phone or my book. I don't know why, but I just didn't. The subway seemed slower that day. As if it were moving through molasses.

That day on the subway, on *my* subway, I felt unsafe. Not in danger, just unsafe. Like my every move could have negative consequences to myself or others. This angers me. Who let this virus make *my* city, the one I grew up wandering around, unsafe? My city was all of a sudden an unsafe place. It was later labelled to be the epicenter of the virus in the United States. *My* city, unsafe places.

Christopher Tamburin, 19
(Dothan, Alabama)

It was March 10, 2020, a normal Monday in New Orleans. The temperature had finally risen from the 50s in the winter to spring's 60s and 70s. Being born and raised in the Deep South, this was ideal. I hated the cold, and even though most people hate the heat and humidity, I was glad to see it finally return.

It's hard to look back and remember how you thought, or how you felt about something when so much has happened since then. At the time, I remember there was a movement of people trying to stop people from treating Asians poorly because of coronavirus. A few cases had been reported in the US, but nothing drastic. I didn't think it was a big deal. I never imagined that we would go into a shutdown.

At 2:00 in the afternoon, I walked into the Woldenburg Art Center for my Chemistry lecture. Professor Lopreore stood at the podium and told us that she was going to teach us how to use Zoom if we got sent home. I laughed it off. COVID was far away and not going to affect us in New Orleans. It seemed strange that we would be preparing this early for it.

March 11, 2020: We hear about a positive case in New Orleans. People start to get antsy. Rumors begin flying, "They're sending us home." I didn't think we would, it was an overreaction. We would be fine, right? Stay on campus, finish out the semester. I pushed all this into the back of my mind. I had two midterms this week. Those were my top priorities now.

March 12, 2020: It's my dad's forty-eighth birthday. I had bought him a college baseball cap for his birthday. Rather than ship it, I was going to give it to him in person when he came to visit in two weeks. It was a pretty day; sunny, 80 degrees with a cool breeze. But if you live in New Orleans, you know how fast the sun can disappear, and the rain can wash away the good feelings and turn them into a cold, miserable day. Again, rumors are flying, nobody can shut up about COVID. I'm just trying to study. At 5:30, the email came. Mike Fitts himself. Evacuations, starting Friday, with everybody gone by the

25th. I was stunned. College was my life, my friends were here, the people who made me feel at home, and it was ripped away from me.

I had to leave later than most. I didn't have the luxury of owning a car or living somewhere where it was convenient to fly. Dothan, Alabama was a five-hour drive, and my parents couldn't get off work on such short notice. So, I waited, watching as all my friends left. Pretty soon, it was just my brother, my friend Francesca, and me. Finally, our family friend, Dennis, came to pick us up. I remember feeling nothing but dread as we drove home. We talked mainly about football on that drive home since Dennis's son played football at Louisville with that season's NFL MVP, Lamar Jackson.

Mr. Dennis was always a good chat.

We made it home, and my mom had prepared a nice dinner for us. I gave my dad his birthday present and we sat down for our family meal. It was a nice meal. However, after living on your own, it's hard to adjust to life back home. Now to find out how to pass the time.

One of the great things about having a twin brother is that with most things you are equally matched. However, we are also super competitive. Mix this with a ping pong table upstairs and you've got your number-one time killer. We spent countless hours upstairs, swinging away on our ping pong table, practicing, improving. Our games got better and better until we were both just going back and forth for hours, determined to win. No sports on TV? It didn't matter. Upstairs at our house, it was first to twenty-one points, best of five games.

If I'm going to remember anything about this quarantine, it's going to be that ping pong table, and the time I spent on it.

Eventually, classes ended and I started working at a fast-food restaurant. To be quite honest, the virus hadn't touched our corner of Alabama, so we had already begun to go back to a sense of normal life. People still wore masks, but it was business as usual. To celebrate the end of classes, we went to the Florida beaches for Memorial Day. We met up with some family friends in hopes of a nice weekend. However, the weekend took a turn for the worst pretty fast.

There was a boy on the beach, who my sister met, and she wanted to get to know him. So, my brother and I concocted a plan where we asked him to teach us how to play spike-ball, and then let our sister play with us. It worked like a charm. Since the water was rough that day, we played spike-ball for hours. It was such a great time until I heard the yelling.

"Oh, shit!" somebody screams.

"Move out of the way!" screams another.

"Is anybody here a doctor? We need a doctor!"

I stand by and watch as five men dragged a lifeless purple corpse from the ocean onto the beach. For twenty minutes, they did CPR but to no avail. I couldn't help but watch in horror at what was happening. Eventually, the EMS showed up and took him to the hospital. I read on the news that he was dead on arrival at the hospital. I was so shaken up, I walked back to the beach house, grabbed my belongings, and just hit the road back to Dothan. That was a rough ride home. Death is not something I ever wanted to see, but life must go on.

Since I had nothing else to do but work, I decided to do an online summer semester of Organic Chemistry. The class started on May 26, with the final on June 26. This month may have been the craziest, most stressful in my life. The lectures: confusing. Labs: unorganized. Tests: impossible. My mental health: struggling. That long month had me on the ropes from the start to the end. When the final rolled around, I had an average of 64% in the class. I had to do well on this final. I studied my ass off for it, only to come out with a 52/150. Thankfully, everybody else did so poorly that this was curved to a B-. It was brutal, but it's over, so what now?

As the fourth of July rolled around, the country was in a place I'd never seen it before. The Black Lives Matter movement had never been stronger since the death of George Floyd and Breonna Taylor (whose murderers had not been arrested as of writing this) had rocked the nation. The young demanded change, while the Boomers dug their heels in the mud and screamed no! Half the nation was ready to celebrate our nation's birthday while others demonized the holiday, calling for change in our country before they could celebrate. I honestly didn't know how to feel. I wanted to celebrate, but it didn't feel right. I felt as if some people were using the fourth to worship the country, and others damn it. I went out with my family to the beach to please my parents, but in my heart, I still didn't know how to feel about the holiday. Soon those feelings wouldn't matter anyway.

Not a day after the fourth, COVID's shadow finally reached Dothan, Alabama. I began to wear a mask to work, where my boss claimed I was worried too much. But it was getting worse. Friends getting sick. Cases rising. For most of the country, this would be the second wave, but it was our first wave. Not three days after I busted out my mask, the health department came in, requiring all food service employees to wear masks. My boss was furious but begrudgingly complied.

At the time I am writing this, it is July 8, 2020. It is my parent's twenty-fifth anniversary today. In my little corner of Alabama, COVID is getting worse by the day, and I am uncertain what is to come. I hope someday we can get back to a sense of normalcy, however, with the storm of COVID, George Floyd, and Kanye's recent bid for president, I don't know if it will be the same ever again. Maybe things won't ever be the same, and maybe that's a good thing. But what do I know? I only hope we come out of this storm stronger and more united than before. I hope we can learn to prevent this from ever happening again.

Maximillian DeLahunta, 18 (Tenafly, New Jersey)

Ironic

Ironic. Probably the last term that I would have thought to use as a description for the summer leading into my freshman year of college, and yet here we are. Gen Z, as my age group is called, is a generation known for a multitude of new peculiar practices, one of the most popular being social media. Every sane parent has warned their kids about the dangers of social media, how it can detach someone from the "real world" and their "real friends".

Here is where we reach the irony in the situation. The world has been forced to recognize the very thing that threatened interpersonal connection itself as the only form of "safe communication". In our current crisis, the standards of what is considered a "normal" way of communicating has changed. Not only is it now "normal" to be in front of a computer to talk to friends all day, as before it was taboo. So, has this in any way changed the manner in which I will enter college? Yes, and here's why.

At the beginning of the global pandemic, I was extremely scared of losing connection with the friends I became close to over my four years in high school. But a thought quickly surfaced, this might have been the best thing to happen to me. I was aware that everyone loses friends after high school. People who you will sit and chat with provided the opportunity, but nobody you wish to maintain any real connection with. By separating from our class, I realized who was important to me and who was going to remain in my life.

Not only did I decide to form stronger relationships with particular friends, but I began to form new connections with future classmates. A group called "Zoom Gang" is a collection of Cornell 2024 students from across the schools that decided to hop on a Zoom call together and just become friends. These are now some of my closest friends to date, bonds strengthened through joint struggle, despite not even having met some of them in person at all. If the world had not come to a metaphorical stop, I may have never been a part of a group that I felt so welcomed into. In a way, it is not too hard for me to find a reason why I am at peace with the state of the world. It's ironic that during a global event that we are all supposed to be socially distanced, that I have never felt so close to so many people.

Cris Eli Blak, 21
(Louisville, Kentucky)

This is the strangest time I think any of us will ever experience in our lives. The world changed in an instant and we had to make a decision: take the risk or stay inside and wait for an invisible killer to disappear. I don't think any amount of reading or watching documentaries about past plagues can help make sense of the one we are living through now.

Still, I tell myself that everything is going to be fine because, well, we have been here before, right? This isn't our first outbreak rodeo. We can get through this. We will get through this. We have to.

Ava Silverman, 18
(Cedar Grove, New Jersey)

I Remember

I remember life before,
days of plenty
and nights adored,
before I was swept up
from golden shore.
Alas, those days
are sadly no more.

I remember tasting pears,
ripe from the market
in the square,
in days before
my falling hair,
Those days are
no longer ours to share.

Painted Wings

When the someone pushes away
the notion that the frost is approaching once more,
Did it ever really exist for them?
Did they experience it in the same way?
Were the bears, bundled in blubber,

and hiding away in hibernation,
as afraid as the butterflies,
whose bodies and wings were burdened by the chill?

When it is easy for one to turn a blind eye to the suffering of others,
it is made simpler to deny that adversities ever existed,
to affirm that they are resolved,
when the harsh truth is that they have just been buried,
beneath the dirt and the snow.
But when the flowers grow,
they are brought back to the surface and felt by the pollinators,
with pretty, painted wings,
fluttering and flying with fear in their hearts,
and guilt for feeling so.

Shahamat Uddin, 21
(Roswell, Georgia)

April 7, 2020

Heartbreak, Coronavirus, and the Best People I've Ever Known

Today, almost three weeks after Tulane's initial announcement of transitioning academic instruction online, I decided to take a walk through campus. I was met with a chilling sadness as I passed through McAlister Place, eyeing the remaining pavement chalk of planned events that will never happen.

Just a few weeks ago, lively and unwary students were filtering in and out of buildings that are now locked, closed off with security guards standing close by. Posters plaster classroom windows instructing our community to maintain social distance. My heart is heavy as I reach Gibson Hall, the end of my campus walk. I look out across the Academic Quad, and there is not a single person in sight.

These days have felt like weeks and these weeks have felt like months, and the moments we were hoping that would last the longest have slipped away from us the quickest. This has been no easy time for any of us. I remember the waves of devastation that hit my peers as they grappled with the coronavirus pandemic.

I sat close to my roommates as they mourned the end of months and months of work—planning the WTUL fiftieth anniversary marathon, the most legendary Crawfest ever expected, an epic Tulane Palestine week—all gone now, stolen with little warning. My best friend called me in tears. She would have to say goodbye to her secret college boyfriend and return to the strict Brown parents who refused to let her speak to him. A freshman I knew was just starting to feel the symptoms of his depression less and less, and now is forced into an immediate confrontation with the place where it all began.

Sunday was the most stunning day for me. Within hours, I lost both my Mid-City server job and post-grad offer. I didn't want to leave my house and say goodbye to anyone; I didn't want to bring this experience to reality at all.

The week following Tulane's announcement was the most difficult. Each hour was characterized by the most atypical kind of uncertainty. Day by day, different friends announced their abrupt decisions to leave New Orleans. Plans that looked like the entire senior class riding out their final semester in the city quickly shifted to lonelier and quieter days until soon, the only people I saw were the people I lived with.

Any attempt at ceremony was distasteful. A drink at The Boot could have meant infection for weeks. The promised goodbye banquets and senior traditions, moments that were years in the making, could not be the special occasions of closure we had hoped for, but were actually deeply serious public health risks.

It was a cruel irony. Our efforts to commemorate one another would certainly increase our potential to hurt one another. Before we knew it, people were gone. All the things left unsaid still linger on my tongue. In my free time, I fantasize about what could have been but then quickly return to worrying about what actually is.

It all just feels like a really bad breakup. Students were ripped away from the promise of lasting final memories, blocked from returning to campus, and told to pack up their things and go. The hurt still stings like an untreated wound. My mind keeps racing, wondering if

I did everything that I could have and if I had known it would be like this, is there anything I would have done differently?

I keep coming back to the people. Yes, I am upset about the events that I won't get to attend, but it's the rushed and absent goodbyes that hurt the most. I had plans, we all had plans, or at least ideas of plans about how our farewells would be, some part of a goodbye that we had control over. But now we don't. We are literally in the middle of a pandemic. Instead of a farewell, it was an "I hope you stay alive".

There was no real closure. Our community and our university can try to do everything they can to give us some virtual feeling of a senior spring sendoff, but the hurt continues because it is not the lifelong planned expectations for a college graduation.

I don't want to look for the silver linings. I didn't want my senior spring to have to turn into something that made me stronger, something I talk about in job interviews, something I laugh about years from now. I just wanted it to be a little close to the farewell I had been looking forward to for twenty-one years.

It is always these things that we don't have any control over that make us feel the most pain. I like to think that I have acquired skills to cope with the heavy things in life that are simply out of my control. Reacting to systems of racism, homophobia, and xenophobia, I look at the things that hurt me, take time to feel the fullest extent of that suffering, and attempt to transform it into some higher pursuit of good, maybe activism. Yet, as I look this pandemic in the face and feel all the pain from things it has taken away from me, I struggle to turn it into any good at all.

It wasn't until a close friend of mine shared an interview with David Kessler, an expert on human reaction to loss, that I was able to fully realize that much of my internal distress surrounding coronavirus was actually a feeling of grief. Three weeks ago, there was a whole future and world ahead of me that I was dead set on living through. Now, it's gone, or at least uncertain, and what I am really left with is grief.

And grief requires grieving. Unfortunately, this is a bitterly long process. I find that there is no way to truly move onto the next stage of my life without feeling and interrogating the sadness that has resulted from this pandemic.

As mere young adults, this seems like one of the most challenging things we will have to do. Every day, I wake up and try to think about life in a new way that makes me feel better. It's like trying on different hats until one feels right, just looking for that perspective that fits just right enough to keep me going forward.

This is much of why I think of the effects of the coronavirus pandemic like heartbreak. I am imagining the entire senior class getting dumped by Tulane all on the same day. It sucks. We don't get our closure, and we didn't do anything to deserve it. Instead, we have our string of broken hearts, wishing things hadn't gone the way that they did. But like the pain of all bad breakups, I know this too shall pass.

Having decided to stay in New Orleans indefinitely, I still walk through campus almost every single day. It is nothing like I have ever seen it before, but on my walks, it feels good to touch a piece of Tulane that makes me happy—the grass on Newcomb Quad, my freshmen dorm, the benches outside of Jones Hall—and remember great times that still would have been great even if I had known my college career would end in an international pandemic.

I have found that life is chock-full of things we cannot control—more often those than the ones we can—and that I can't always make an enemy of the things that hurt me. But it is from the things that hurt me that I am able to find the things that make me the most happy.

(Courtesy of the Tulane Hullabaloo)

CONCLUSION

What It Has Meant to Be a Part of This Book

From the compilers...

Gabriella, 10

I was proud of myself to be able to share my story and to connect with other kids from around the country. I'm thankful for this unique opportunity.

Sam, 12

This book has been great to be a part of. It's had me do really deep thinking about this virus and time period. Everyone will get to see all kids' perspectives from different areas of America. I think this book will be very interesting and I am excited to see what people think of it.

Lena, 12

The book has impacted me deeply. It helped me learn that I am not alone in missing big sporting events, summer trips, and birthday parties. Kids are sharing the grief of not having a normal life right now. I have gratitude...and feel that coming out of this pandemic I will be doing my best to keep achieving my goals.

Josephine and Norah, 13

It was really nice to put our words on paper and know that some people will read kids' perspectives about the pandemic. Not many adults listen to what kids have to say or even care about their thoughts. Being a part of this book helped us realize that instead of being helpless, there are ways you can stand up and make your voice heard. There are always things you can do to make action in the world, and this book helped us realize that.

Teddy, 13

This book means more to me than just being able to have the title of "published author". It has been a fun experience that will resonate in my memory forever. Our writing can be a representation to many people in the future of what life was like living through COVID-19. A disease of this magnitude has almost never happened before, and I hope it never happens again. Maybe our words will teach people about how coronavirus shocked the world. I am honored to be able to say that I was a part of this book.

Kaleigh, 14

Writing and becoming a part of this book has given me a chance to see how other people have dealt with this pandemic. I have learned how others are struggling and coping during these times. Writing in this book has shown me that everyone has their strengths and weaknesses, but I have yet to figure out mine. I am grateful that I and my close friend got involved with something very special. I hope that everyone that was a part of this book can stay healthy and get through these tough times.

Hailey, 14

Finally having my voice heard, and that of many others, gives me strength. After months of uncertainty and not knowing how to feel, being a part of this publication has given me a sense of connection. When I was told I would not have a graduation, it was devastating. It helped to hear from the writings of others who also missed theirs. Overall, being a part of this book has meant a lot to me and given me a sense of closure.

James, 17

Participating in a book like this is a certain way for the largely unheard voices of American youth to be heard. It seems that adults love to tell us that "everything will be okay", even when it is a blatant lie. Rather, adults do what they think is best, without consulting the youth. Obviously, there are reasons for this; children are typically less informed on current circumstances. However, that does not mean that our opinions and needs should be disregarded. While adults are dealing with the current disaster, they should also realize that it is us, not them, who will live to deal with the legacy of COVID-19 and their decisions.

Sophie, 17

Our world is broken, right now so many insane things are going on, this virus leading them. Our stories vary depending on where we live, where we go to school, what activities we are allowed to do, and so much more. For me, being a part of this book has been an eye-opening experience in which I've learned about different peoples' perspectives on quarantine life. We all share the commonality of dealing with the pandemic, the connections to others' stories that I could relay back to my own life. I hope this book gives readers the ability to connect the way I have.

Tess, 18

For me, participating in this book was a new experience. It wasn't really what I thought I would be doing during my quarantine. I would say that I am really happy that I was able to put my experiences during this crazy time into words that other people can hopefully read and relate to. Being a part of this project has been super influential for me because I realized how much I enjoyed writing my stories and how I should participate in more projects like this. I also feel like this project was entirely out of my comfort zone, which for me is definitely a big task to accomplish because I'm not the kind of person who generally feels out of their comfort zone and so I definitely think that it was great for me to get out of my comfort zone a bit. Overall, I really enjoyed participating in this project and hope that I can participate in another similar project.

Aidan, 19

History is easily misinterpreted, misremembered, manipulated, and, at worst, completely changed or forged. Being a part of this compilation has meant the history being made by my peers and me will be accurately recorded and remembered. The diversity of compilers and contributors furthers that sentiment; my own story and perspective on the pandemic, along with scores of other young people, are vital to understanding the vast scope of coronavirus, and I'm grateful for the opportunity to participate.

Nate, 19

Being part of YPOP has had a big impact in my life. The pandemic has changed the way that I view a lot of things in the world, major or minor. I am incredibly excited to see the book get put out and be able to read words of my own alongside words of others that have experienced things similar to what I have experienced. It was an experience I wouldn't change, and one I'll remember forever.

Sofia Haskel, 19 (Chief Compiler)

Being part of this team has not only kept me busy during quarantine, but it has led me to discover a thriving passion for writing. I have learned that during times of hardship, whether internal or external, documentation can alleviate the burden. This is what we are doing now by putting together an anthology during the COVID-19 crisis. I am so grateful to be a part of a project that will be remembered in history and that will spread feelings of warmth and empathy to whoever reads it.

Sophia Larson, 19 (Assistant Editor)

When I was contacted about being a part of this book, the full weight of the pandemic had just set in. It was a few weeks after I'd been sent home from college. Until that point, I was under the impression that the pandemic would mean a prolonged spring break, nothing more. I was under the impression that there were people who were capable of flattening the curve. I was under the impression that life as I knew it would return sooner rather than later.

I was wrong. I was optimistic until the last, but finally the email came: I would not be resuming school this semester.

Then, Nancy got in contact with me. At a time when I was feeling so much loss, an opportunity emerged from the darkness. Though I could not fight the virus directly, I could put my energy into something productive. This project is something to capture the moment where so many people across the country are feeling the same sense of loss that I was feeling. The things we'd taken for granted—our health, our education, our friends, our jobs—were being taken from us, one by one. In a time when people (especially our young people) feel so powerless, what else is there to do but write?

Nancy S. Nelson (Editor)

Six months ago, I could never have imagined that I would be publishing a book with the help of young people from all over the country. I was thrust into this project at full speed. Soon, twenty submissions turned into fifty, which turned into one hundred and twenty-five. In total, we compiled over forty-thousand words in less than four months during a worldwide pandemic...unbelievable!

This anthology began with nineteen compilers who agreed to write two written pieces and to collect the writings of two or three friends from a US state other than their own. On June 3, the group (which I have fondly referred to as "Team YPOP") met on Zoom for the first time. Except for one of my grandchildren and two other youngsters, I had never personally met any of the other participants. As we introduced ourselves, it hit me that these young people were as enthusiastic as I was at the prospect of creating this book. In six weeks of meetings, with one forty-minute session per week, we collected over one hundred and forty submissions from thirty-eight states.

At today's final YPOP meeting, everyone was given ten minutes to write an answer to the question, "What has being a part of this book meant to you?" For me, I could fill many pages on all my thoughts. What began as a vague idea in my head has become an amazing reality, thanks to the incredible work of young writers. While enduring school closings, personal tragedies, canceled life events, isolation from friends and relatives, and fears of the unknown, the contributors in all age groups submitted their writing in a myriad of creative formats. The result is a book to be proud of.

I believe the ingenuity that fills these pages comes not merely from talent, but from the willingness to express emotion and opinion from the heart. The honest effort to overcome trauma with resilience is also evident in every written piece presented in this book. There is much hope to be glimpsed in the writings, which represent the voices of those who will be responsible for leading the world to a better place.

Wherever this compilation goes and whoever chooses to read it, these tales of extreme crisis need to be told among the many who will follow throughout history. My hope is that readers find the same inspiration that I have absorbed while editing this book during a very bleak time. In my professional and personal life, I have rarely had a more rewarding experience. I will therefore be forever grateful for the opportunity to present the literary work of so many young people of the pandemic.

July 15, 2020

ACKNOWLEDGMENTS

It is the courageous creativity of the young contributors through-out the United States which has inspired and motivated me. Their writing propelled me forward in the course of compiling this book, and in enduring the early months of the pandemic. I wish I could cite every one of the ten- to twenty-one-year-olds who sent in their submissions.

My gratitude goes to those friends and family who entrusted me with their precious children and grandchildren: Kay Shortway, Andrea Girard, Gail Evans, Juliet Rose Larson, Kay Murcer, Jill Haskel, Jennifer Katz, Andrea Eastaugh, William Cooper, Dr. Mara Gleckel, and Fran Klingenstein. My thanks also to the supportive and enthusiastic parents I met along the way: Bob Bickford, Christina Chiu, Stacy Gonzalez, Laura Martin, Klara Hegedus, Julianna Caplan, Patricia Freund, Shona Tuckman, and Tori Witherspoon.

During my years as a clinical art therapist, there have been many people who taught me the great value in listening to young people. Some of them are: Frances Tellner (Director of Child Life, New York Presbyterian Hospital), Jeanne Sweeney, Rosemary Petruzzi, and CB Bucknor. And for all those hospital workers and childcare providers whom I had the privilege of working alongside, my gratitude and well wishes go out to you.

Even while dealing with their own personal and professional issues during the pandemic, there were special people who offered encour-agement and advice: Andrew and Mary Hendry; Janine Baron; Blair Schwartz, PsyD; Chester Rothstien; Edie Shane Amster; Eloise

Johnson; Martine Gerard; John Duff; Susan Newman, PhD; Dawn Bolt; Nancy Wolk, PsyD; Libby Rappaport; Anthony Zaccardi; and Sophie Barschi.

And finally, to Sofia and Sophia, and the YPOP Team of Gen Z people, whom I am so happy to have virtually met and worked with for this book's compilation.

About the Editor

Nancy S. Nelson, M.S. ATR is a Creative Arts Therapist who lives and works in New York City. Trained at Mount Sinai Hospital, she served for sixteen years on the staff of The Child Life Center, Department of Pediatrics at New York Hospital-Cornell Medical Center. Nancy is a graduate of Columbia University and received her master's degree from The College of New Rochelle. For forty years, she has maintained a private practice in art therapy and psychotherapy. She has authored two previous books: *The Doodle Dictionary* (Doubleday, 1992) and *The Doodle Diary* (Random House, 2008).

Partial proceeds from the sale of this book
will be donated to:
Save the Children Coronavirus Response Fund
United Negro College Fund Scholarships
The American Art Therapy Association

Made in the USA
Columbia, SC
03 March 2021